California Maritime Academy
Vallejo, California

1. All pupils in the school are entitled to use the library and to draw books.
2. Reference books, such as encyclopedias and dictionaries, are to be used only in the library.
3. Reserved books may be borrowed for one period, or at the close of school, and should be returned before the first class the following school day.
4. All other books may be retained for two weeks.
5. Two cents a day is charged for each book kept overtime.
6. Injury to books beyond reasonable wear and all losses shall be paid for.
7. No books may be taken from the library without being charged.

TWENTIETH CENTURY INTERPRETATIONS
OF

PRIDE AND PREJUDICE

A Collection of Critical Essays

Edited by

E. RUBINSTEIN

Prentice-Hall, Inc. *Englewood Cliffs, N. J.*

Current printing (last number):
10 9 8 7 6 5 4 3 2 1

PRENTICE-HALL INTERNATIONAL, INC. (*London*)
PRENTICE-HALL OF AUSTRALIA, PTY. LTD. (*Sydney*)
PRENTICE-HALL OF CANADA, LTD. (*Toronto*)
PRENTICE-HALL OF INDIA PRIVATE LTD. (*New Delhi*)
PRENTICE-HALL OF JAPAN, INC. (*Tokyo*)

A Note on Texts and References

The standard, indispensable text of *Pride and Prejudice* is that established by R. W. Chapman in Volume II of his *Novels of Jane Austen,* 3rd ed. (London: Oxford University Press, 1932); many critical studies, in citing the novel, refer directly to page numbers in this edition. Since, however, most students will not be working from the Oxford edition, such a method of reference here seems pointless. Hence I have, in all cases where the essay provides page references, added in brackets chapter references as well so that any given passage can, with a little effort, be located in any edition of the novel. Thus a quotation from the last paragraph of the novel might be followed by "(388 [III, xix])"—page 388 of the Oxford edition, or Volume III, chapter xix. (Since I wish to keep the essays in this volume as close as possible to what their authors intended them to be, I have not added specific references in those essays that did not originally include them.)

Now, some modern editions do not follow Jane Austen's original in dividing the novel into three volumes, but instead number chapters consecutively from the beginning. In this case, a small mathematical calculation is called for. If the passage in question is given as occurring in Volume II, the reader must add 23 to the chapter number in order to find it in a consecutively numbered edition: for example, "II, vi" equals chapter xxix. If the passage occurs in Volume III, the reader must add 42, so that "III, iii" becomes xlv.

I recognize that all this may seem a bit cumbersome, but since there are literally dozens of reprints of the novel available throughout the world, no simpler method presents itself.

Contents

Introduction

by E. Rubinstein

I. Miss Austen, Aunt Jane, and the Author of Pride and Prejudice

To summarize the life of Jane Austen is to risk telling a very dull story indeed; I shall be brief. She was born on December 16, 1775, in the village of Steventon in Hampshire, the seventh of eight children (six male and two female) of the Reverend George Austen and his wife Cassandra. She lived in Steventon until 1801, when her father retired to the spa city of Bath. There he died in 1805, and in the following year Jane Austen moved with her mother and sister to Southampton. In 1809, the three moved once again, this time to another Hampshire village, Chawton, where Jane Austen remained until shortly before her death on July 18, 1817. She was buried in Winchester Cathedral. She never married, nor is there persuasive evidence to indicate that her celibacy was the result of disappointment in love. Though she read widely, she had no formal literary training. She enjoyed virtually no connections with the literary society of her time. Most of her life was given over to her family—to her parents, of course; to her beloved sister Cassandra, who like herself remained unmarried; to her brothers and their many children; and to numerous more distant relations. She appears to have inspired warm affection among those who knew her best, and especially among her nephews and nieces, to whom she was in turn especially devoted. She was, by all accounts, earnest in the practice of the Anglican faith. And that, in outline at least, is about all there is to tell—except to add, by way of testimony to the perversity of genius, that she also happened to write six of the most brilliant novels in the English language.

Needless to say, a life passed in voluntary obscurity is likely to leave a somewhat indistinct record at best, so that, beyond a handful of dates, we know relatively little of the actualities of the writing of Jane Austen's novels. Though we may feel certain, for example, that the book called *Pride and Prejudice* published in 1813 represents a fundamental revision of the book called *First Impressions* completed in 1797, we cannot show with any conclusiveness exactly what was

changed, or even whether some of the alterations had been effected or
at least planned much earlier, perhaps during the ostensibly infertile
period of 1801 to 1809.[1] Our ignorance of these particulars is, however, only symptomatic of our general lack of access to the inner life
of one of the few indisputably major figures among our earlier novelists. In brief, the first and major problem faced by any biographer of
Jane Austen is that of discovering the author of the novels—the
author whom more than one critic has placed next to Shakespeare—
amid the activities of an amiable but wholly unextraordinary maiden
lady, and I do not mean to disparage the talents of the many who
have attempted the task when I offer the opinion that none has quite
succeeded. Here, as illustration of the difficulties involved, is an example of Jane Austen in her domestic role, writing to her sister during
one of their infrequent periods of separation. This letter was written,
I should add, at the very time when her creative powers were approaching their zenith, when, perhaps still occupied with reworking *Pride
and Prejudice* for the press, she was already well at work on her next
novel, *Mansfield Park:*

> Chawton Thursday June 6 [1811]
>
> By this time my dearest Cassandra, you know Martha's plans. I was
> rather disappointed I confess to find that she could not leave Town till
> after ye 24th, as I had hoped to see you here the week before. The de-
> lay however is not great, & everything seems generally arranging itself for
> your return very comfortably. I found Henry perfectly pre-disposed to
> bring you to London if agreable to yourself; he has not fixed his day for
> *going* into Kent, but he must be back again before ye 20th.—You may
> therefore think with something like certainty of the close of your God-
> mersham visit, & will have I suppose about a week for Sloane St. He
> travels in his Gig—& should the weather be tolerable, I think you must
> have a delightful Journey. . . . We are very sorry for the disappointment
> you have all had in Lady B's illness;—but a division of the proposed party
> is with you by this time, & I hope may have brought you a better account
> of the rest.—Give my Love & Thanks to Harriot;—who has written me
> charming things of your looks, & diverted me very much by poor Mrs.
> C. Milles's continued perplexity.—I had a few lines from Henry on
> Tuesday. . . .[2]

I have not selected unfairly: these sentences are quite characteristic
both of Jane Austen's epistolary style and of the customary matter of

---

[1] Such information as we possess is most readily available in R. W. Chapman,
Jane Austen: Facts and Problems (Oxford: Clarendon Press, 1949).

[2] R. W. Chapman, ed., *Jane Austen's Letters to Her Sister Cassandra and Others*,
2nd ed. (London: Oxford University Press, 1952), pp. 288–89. Jane Austen's spelling
and punctuation in her letters are extraordinarily free; I forego the use of *sic* even
at those points where she does greatest violence to modern usage.

her letters. To be sure, she is sometimes more grave, sometimes more caustic, sometimes more concerned with what she is saying and therefore more scrupulous about the way she says it. Indeed, in going through Jane Austen's extant correspondence one even comes upon certain letters (most of them quoted in the essays reprinted in this volume) in which, however triflingly, with whatever degree of uneasy self-depreciation, she talks revealingly about her role as novelist. But such letters are exceptions. Rarely would anyone scanning Jane Austen's letters be shaken from the assumption that here is a woman whose interests are entirely definable in terms of who will visit whom, where, when, and wearing what clothes. Granted, it would be unusual to find in any casual correspondence the serious commitments and intricate linguistic strategies that proclaim the great works of literature. But it is just as unusual, I think, to find any writer as gifted as Jane Austen obscuring at every turn the traits of astuteness and imagination that we identify with her novels.

Here, to introduce Jane Austen in her other role, are the celebrated opening sentences of *Pride and Prejudice:*

> It is a truth universally acknowledged, that a single man in possession of a good fortune, must be in want of a wife.
>
> However little known the feelings or views of such a man may be on his first entering a neighbourhood, this truth is so well fixed in the minds of the surrounding families, that he is considered as the rightful property of some one or other of their daughters.
>
> "My dear Mr. Bennet," said his lady to him one day, "have you heard that Netherfield Park is let at last?"

Not a few critics of the novel (including several of those whose essays are included in this volume) have had a go at this passage. What I would myself like to call attention to—borrowing in part from Dorothy Van Ghent—is the extraordinary verbal ingenuity it exhibits, a quality that most of Jane Austen's letters, along with her family's doting recollections, would let go largely unsuspected.

Consider the many tactical functions of the first sentence. It is now a commonplace to point to the way in which the "truth universally acknowledged" flows immediately and naturally into the specific narrative situation from which the novel is to grow. But we must also attend to the tone. The first half-dozen words announce not only a vast range of practical experience and practical wisdom on the part of the narrator but also a confidence and finality bordering on smugness. Yet almost at once a process of ironic deflation sets in, as the grand "universally" passes into the question of a mere "neighbourhood," which in turn passes into the voice of a single—and unusually fatuous—representative of one little "neighbourhood" in particular. Are we being asked to smile at the emptiness of facile generalization? The question is one that is not without immediate relevance to the story of Elizabeth and Darcy, both of whom have a habit of seeing that which is only provisional, and often half-true, as final. Like Darcy's original notion of Elizabeth's plainness and insignificance, and Elizabeth's of Darcy's irremediable haughtiness, the opening sentence simply misrepresents the actual state of things: neither of the rich unmarried gentlemen we encounter in the story is in fact so actively seeking a wife. Despite what the opening sentence proclaims (or rather, in perfect accordance with what it proclaims *ironically*), it is up to the ladies to make marriages happen. We should notice that the terms of proprietorship and control, at first identified with the male (who is "in possession" of his "good fortune") almost immediately shift to the female (whose "property"—indeed, *"rightful* property" he becomes); and the further defeat of the male is suggested by "surrounding families," which, with its connotation of organized entrapment, harks back to the sense of coercion first articulated in the *"must* be" of the rhetorically inexhaustible opening sentence.

Nor is this all. As Mrs. Van Ghent reminds us, many of the key words ("fortune," "property," maybe even "well fixed") serve to locate the activities of courtship and marriage at the level of business transactions. But is the reader meant to accept without qualification this dehumanized vision? Is he to condone the indiscriminate ambition, the failure to heed individual differences and individual needs, implicit not only in "However little known [or considered!] the feelings and views of such a man" but also in the offhanded "some one or other of their daughters"? Of course not—no more than he is meant to accept at face value the incongruously chivalric phrase "his lady" (why not simply "his wife"?) that serves to introduce the hopeless marital situation of the Bennets. All the language of these sentences is meant to alert us to the dangers of the game of courtship—its brutalizing economic stresses (think of poor Charlotte Lucas) and, in the figures of the Bennets, the ghastly punishment meted out to those who play it foolishly. To sum it all up, then, such a passage invites the reader to experience the English language in a state of remarkable concentration, words pressed to yield up every possible drop of sardonic commentary. In the shortest possible time, an entire verbal environment has been made, a whole system of values both asserted and tacitly challenged. "Aunt Jane" used a very different pen when she wrote for the world.

My first point, then, is this: the achievement of *Pride and Prejudice* cannot be explained satisfactorily either in terms of young Miss Austen of Steventon,[3] who wrote the draft of a novel called *First Impressions,* or of middle-aged Aunt Jane of Chawton, who revised and published it under its now-familiar title. It would, of course, be foolish to pretend that a reader can (or even, in most cases, should) avoid the natural tendency to attempt to adjust what he knows of an author's life to what he discovers in the author's books. To encounter a great work of art is to be exposed to the presence of a great artist, and engagement with the former must necessarily provoke, at the very least, a certain degree of curiosity about the latter. And, though one can never explain unusual talent as the simple result of identifiable psychological causes or predict the range of a writer's work on the basis of the range of his documentable experience, still one can, in most instances, bring biographical data into some kind of meaningful accord with literary performance. But when, as with Jane Austen, the very attempt encourages simplification and distortion of the writing itself—especially if the reader is unschooled in the perilous art of biographical criticism—then it is wise to give over the effort. The best advice any reader of *Pride and Prejudice* can follow is first to experience the book on its own terms, with all the attention it calls for; and then, only then, to turn to Jane Austen's letters and the reminiscences of her family—less for their very infrequent insights into the novels than for a sense of the virtuosity with which she managed to balance the two major claims on her attention: her family and her writing. If we expect the Austens to provide relatively little in the way of excitement, and still less in the way of deeper awareness of Jane Austen the novelist, we are in a better position to understand why the author of *Pride and Prejudice* found them such a captivating group.

II. True but Trivial?

Erroneous assumptions based on what we know of Jane Austen's life are not the only source of the tendency—a common one, unfortunately—to minimize her accomplishments as a novelist. The accusation most regularly brought against her work is that its concerns are relatively trivial. From the earliest reviewers to very recent critics, one complaint—and a complaint it remains, however richly framed by words of the highest praise—is heard again and again: "What she

---

[3] According to the usage of the day, she would probably have been known to those well acquainted with her family as "Miss Jane Austen" or "Miss Jane," since only the eldest unmarried daughter always took the family name. Thus Jane Bennet is "Miss Bennet," Elizabeth Bennet often "Miss Elizabeth."

does, she does well, perhaps better than anyone—though of course we all know that there is so much more to life and to literature than this."

And indeed there *is* much more than *Pride and Prejudice* explores. But then there is also much more than we find in the poems of Donne or of Yeats, or in *Crime and Punishment* or *A Portrait of the Artist As a Young Man,* or even in any single play of Shakespeare, yet few critics feel obliged to dwell upon the "limitations" of any of these. The difference arises at least in part because that which Jane Austen elects to leave out (or appears to) is precisely that which, according to our inherited judgments of moral and intellectual worth, is most nearly crucial to any proper understanding of the human situation: (1) a view of man's mortality, expressed in theological or existential terms; (2) a view of man's ultimate earthly destiny, as explicitly articulated in the language of social and political valuation; (3) a view of man's most profound personal compulsion (next to his instinct for survival), his sexuality. So acutely felt is the absence of these familiar emphases that even commentators who, like Mark Schorer and Mrs. Van Ghent, find *Pride and Prejudice* wholly congenial and admirable, have nonetheless thought it necessary to begin with statements about the careful and deliberate choice on the author's part that determined the novel's limitations. In so doing, of course, they make valuable points. It is most important to stress that a strong sense of what, misleadingly or not, is called classicism, manifest in the shape and balance of the novel itself, caused Jane Austen to find great satisfaction in achieving so much within rigidly circumscribed bounds. It is correct, too, to stress that what is left out of *Pride and Prejudice* does not necessarily signal a lack of experience on the author's part, since, as Mrs. Van Ghent reminds us, even the relatively slender biographical evidence at our disposal is enough to assure us that Jane Austen was exposed to many aspects of life not incorporated into her novels. Still, one cannot but wonder whether these apologies are strictly necessary.

First of all, though it is true that in *Pride and Prejudice* the processes of aging and dying lie far from the center of things, is this not always the case in romantic comedy, of which *Pride and Prejudice* is certainly an instance? Their absence, as I shall suggest more fully in the third section of this Introduction, is largely a question of genre, and it is foolish to ask of any work that it deal with concerns that are no part of its mode and that would indeed subvert its own carefully chosen emphases.

Second, while Jane Austen does not explicitly dwell on matters of social and political history, these do provide the ambience of her work. When Mr. Schorer affirms that the social setting of all her novels "is one in which a feudalistic order that does not know that it is dying and a bourgeois or mercantile order that is not yet confident that it is quite alive, meet and conflict and sometimes merge," [4] he is rightly drawing attention to the nature of the opposing energies that animate the plot and to the size of the shadows that Jane Austen's little "neighbourhood" throws on the screen of an attentive reader's imagination. The initial hostility, gradual reconciliation, and final union of Elizabeth and Darcy represent the social history of Jane Austen's England writ small, for the challenge laid to the aristocracy by a newly effectual middle class, and the inevitable assimilation of the former by the latter, are among the crucial facts of European social history from the eighteenth century to the twentieth. In other words, Jane Austen's manner of communicating the larger pressures that determine and modify the behavior of her characters is purely novelistic and dramatic; the small world she creates is precisely that —a world, albeit in small.

Finally, as to the sexuality: if its physical manifestations are not directly represented, its social implications surely are. The novel makes clear, in the figure of Charlotte Lucas, that to give oneself to a man without desire, to accede to a polite form of prostitution, is to sacrifice what is most valuable in the self, and, in the figure of Mr. Bennet, that to submit to lust, or even to a giddy impulse (why else would Mr. Bennet have selected the bride he did?) is to forego the possibility of rational happiness. In the figure of Wickham we see male attractiveness ruthlessly employed as a commodity for self-advancement, working its deadly effect upon those least able to resist, the mindless Lydia and the nervously uncertain Miss Darcy. Thus, if the sexual aspects of romantic attraction remain, according to certain moral and literary conventions of Jane Austen's time, unspoken, this does not mean that when young men and women consider and discuss each other they are thinking only of eventual family portraits. *Pride and Prejudice* takes place in a world less eager than our own—or Chaucer's, or Shakespeare's—to introduce sexuality into the province of literary language; but it is hardly fair to say that any novel whose denouement depends upon a seduction is prudish.

Still, to the extent that a work as intricate and various as *Pride and Prejudice* can be said to be "about" any one subject, that subject would not be sexuality but rather its social expression, courtship; and it may at first seem to a modern reader that such a subject cannot warrant the fierce scrutiny that *Pride and Prejudice* accords it.

[4] "Pride Unprejudiced," *The Kenyon Review*, XVIII (Winter, 1956), 80.

Once again, however, we come up against received and unevaluated assumptions. Even in our own time, when a far greater degree of sexual freedom is permitted and when laws governing divorce are incomparably less rigid, the choice of a husband remains for most young women the single most fundamental and far-reaching of life's decisions, while even for men the selection of a wife is challenged in importance only by the selection of a profession. To Jane Austen and her contemporary audience, the subject of courtship was absolutely central, and it necessarily remained so because it was involved both with the social perpetuation of the family line through inherited property and with that larger interpenetration of social classes already mentioned. The state of marriage was, in addition, the *sine qua non* of a tolerable existence, as Charlotte Lucas would be the first to remind us. But what gave the subject excitement as well as importance was the responsibility of the female herself in the choice of her husband. The freedom allowed the English girl in courtship was enough to astonish many contemporary observers from countries in which marriages between respectable young people were usually arranged quite without reference to the desires of those most directly concerned, and more than one Continental visitor to Jane Austen's England has left testimony to the fact that the period of courtship was, for the English girl, a moment of unique adventure, the one time in her life when her destiny lay not in her family's hands, or in her husband's, but to a significant degree in her own.

At the risk of ignoring my own caveat against approaching Jane Austen's novels through Aunt Jane, I wish to look briefly now at one of her rarely quoted letters to her favorite niece:

Chawton Feb: 20 [1817]

My dearest Fanny,

   You are inimitable, irresistable. You are the delight of my Life. Such Letters, such entertaining Letters as you have lately sent!—Such a description of your queer little heart!—Such a lovely display of what Imagination does.—You are worth your weight in Gold, or even in the new Silver Coinage.—I cannot express to you what I have felt in reading your history of yourself, how full of Pity & Concern & Admiration & Amusement I have been. You are the Paragon of all that is Silly & Sensible, common-place & eccentric, Sad & Lively, Provoking & Interesting. —Who can keep pace with the fluctuations of your Fancy, the Caprizios of your Taste, the Contradictions of your Feelings?—You are so odd!—& all the time, so perfectly natural—so peculiar in yourself, & yet so like everybody else!—It is very, very gratifying to me to know you so intimately. You can hardly think what a pleasure it is to me, to have such thorough pictures of your Heart.—Oh! what a loss it will be when you are married. You are too agreable in your single state, too agreable as a

Neice. I shall hate you when your delicious play of Mind is all settled
down into conjugal & maternal affections.[5]

It is precisely this "delicious play of Mind" that furnishes a principal
ingredient in Jane Austen's novels. If we know Elizabeth Bennet as
"intimately" as the novelist knew her niece, it is in part because the
"thorough pictures" of her "Heart" were drawn at the one time of
her life when all her skills of judgment and all her sense of ethical
value were inevitably called into play. Jane Austen's repeated use
of the device of courtship was therefore far more than an attempt
to find easy favor with readers of fiction by offering them the "love
interest" they expected. It was the means whereby to examine the
ambitions and trials of the human spirit at a critical moment and in
terms of a specific social world.

In *Pride and Prejudice*, as if to underscore the already considerable
dramatic potential of courtship, Jane Austen magnifies her protagonist's need for accurate perception, moral awareness, and self-knowl-
edge by removing the principal prop on which she might rely, the
aid and advice of parents. It has frequently been remarked that none
of Jane Austen's heroines can look to her parents (in some cases surrogate parents) for much in the way of useful guidance, and Elizabeth
provides a perfect case in point. Mindless Mrs. Bennet lacks the natural equipment even to understand her daughter's needs, let alone
to sympathize with her scruples. Mr. Bennet, on the other hand, may
possess the intelligence and the sympathy, but instead of providing
counsel and discipline, he chooses to hide behind his shield of brittle
irony. Inadequately prepared by her elders for the great adventure
of courtship, inadequately supported during its unfolding, Elizabeth
(like her sister Jane) must look entirely to herself as she negotiates
the stormy channel between the Scylla of spinsterhood and the
Charybdis of a disastrous marriage.

The date of the letter cited above is worth noting. On February 20,
1817, Jane Austen was already in poor health, in fact within six
months of death. But even had her physical condition been better,
she could not reasonably have looked forward to a life of anything
but incurable spinsterhood, for she was a pretty hopeless forty-one
years old. Thus marriage could no longer have claimed the immediate
personal concern it doubtless had had when she began writing fiction,
and biographical considerations once again fail to explain the artist's
choice of subject. Yet, a mature woman in mature control of a unique
talent, she still centered her work upon the activities of young women
faced with the exigencies of finding and marrying the right man. To

[5] *Letters*, pp. 478–79.

be sure, by the time of her last completed novel, *Persuasion*, she invented a heroine closer to thirty than to twenty, and, as Virginia Woolf and others have pointed out, she seemed to be tiring of the familiar matter of the novels. In fact, in the late fragment called *Sanditon* she hints at something very different from her earlier work.[6] But the traditional subject of courtship had served her long and well, and nowhere more brilliantly than in *Pride and Prejudice*.

III. Novel and Comedy

Though we may assume from the quality of the book that the author of *Pride and Prejudice* took her work very seriously indeed, we cannot be certain of the extent to which she consciously understood and planned it in relation to the genre of the novel, born less than a century before her own time. Consciously meditated or not, however, her contribution was significant.

Modern fiction, as it developed in the essentially Calvinist-capitalist England of the eighteenth century,[7] demanded that the reader accept neither monarchs nor heroes nor saints but rather the recognizable, unextraordinary individual as the subject of the writer's most intense moral and psychological explorations. It demanded further that the crises of everyday living be regarded as the best focus of insight not only into character but into higher moral meaning. To a degree unprecedented in Western literature, men and women in the middle station of life—the social and intellectual peers of those who read their stories—moved toward the center of poem, of play, and above all of fictional narrative. Even so, none of Jane Austen's major predecessors in the novel took upon himself the full implications of the genre, for none was able wholeheartedly to accept the everyday world as the boundary of his imagination. Fielding tended always toward the epic, even in a "domestic" novel like *Amelia*; while Defoe's predileciton for the extraordinary and the criminal, Richardson's for intrigue and violence, and Sterne's for wildly eccentric behavior, all left the field of the ostensibly commonplace open for Jane Austen. Though Maria Edgeworth and Fanny Burney anticipated her in some respects, neither had her genius for illuminating the quotidian or her unwavering reliance upon ordinary social intercourse as the indispensable clue to the ways of the spirit. Jane Austen was the first Eng-

---

[6] Virginia Woolf, "Jane Austen," in *The Common Reader* (New York: Harcourt, Brace & World, Inc., 1925), pp. 191–206.

[7] The classic study of the social and philosophical origins of modern fiction is Ian Watt, *The Rise of the Novel* (London: Chatto & Windus Ltd., 1957).

lish writer to confront forthrightly the intrinsic challenges of the form in which she operated.

The new emphasis placed on the circumstances of everyday life by the English novelists before Jane Austen was accompanied by a new emphasis on individual understanding. Fixed systems of "truth" tended to give way to less rigid visions of experience. The central figure in the fiction tended to become the definitive source of his own principal awarenesses, and the drama of the novel tended to be based, to a hitherto unknown extent, upon the clash of incompatible personal visions of the world. The technical challenge that Jane Austen therefore faced (as E. M. Halliday explains in far greater detail in the selection included in this volume) was that of focusing on the mind of at least one central character while at the same time allowing that character's world and its many inhabitants to impose themselves independently upon the reader's attention.

From none of her more distinguished predecessors in the art of the novel could Jane Austen borrow a method entirely suited to these needs. In Defoe's novels, the central figure recounts his story long after the fact. This method threatens always to create too ambiguous a relation between the reader and the narrator-hero by suggesting a considerable distance between the narrator in time present (as he tells the tale) and the narrator in time past (as he participated in the events themselves). More seriously, it significantly limits the possibility of the narrator's reporting with authority upon the processes of any mind but his own. Sterne's technique, that of a disjunctive monologue, not quite internal yet not quite directed to a specific audience, was ideally suited to his own demonstration of the essential incoherence of the human mind, but this was hardly Jane Austen's interest. What is more, she could have had little use for a prose style that precluded, as Sterne's deliberately did, the clear representation of a flow of external events in their chronological order. She was much more seriously attracted to Richardson's technique of telling his story exclusively through personal letters written in the very heat of first-hand experience, and she experimented with it widely in her early writings, but she came to recognize that it did not suit her, perhaps because of its too patent artificiality. Fielding—who, shifting the stress from the mental operations of his central figures, made of the detached and ironic narrator of his novels the only fully developed consciousness to be encountered in them—also exerted an influence upon Jane Austen, but his procedure inevitably signaled a narrator who not only tells but fabricates the tale, willfully manipulating the characters for his own purposes and thus underscoring their fictitiousness.

The narrative method that Jane Austen herself arrived at in the final version of *Pride and Prejudice* will probably seem so familiar and so natural to the modern reader that he may need to be reminded that it was, if not invented, at least perfected by her, before being absorbed into the mainstream of English fiction. The method is this. Assuming (like Fielding) the voice of a wholly authoritative narrator, potentially free to move at will anywhere in time and space, and in and out of the mind of any character, Jane Austen at the same time chooses to focus on the consciousness of one central figure, from whose point of view the narrative is for the most part experienced. Hence she could enjoy, in Ian Watt's phrase, "the advantages both of realism of representation and realism of assessment, of the internal and of the external approaches to character." [8] This is to say that she could demonstrate not only Elizabeth's clear perception of the appearances of Darcy's conduct (and of her own) but at the same time that fundamental if uncertain attraction between them which in large part gives rise to all their misleading behavior and which the reader is permitted to divine before Elizabeth herself. Like all literary techniques, this one has its disadvantages—disadvantages that, one must add, underscore the apparently "limited" scope of the novel. Most aspects of experience that Elizabeth could not witness (private conversations among men, to take a minor but frequently noted illustration) tend to be excluded. But it would be hard to overstate the importance of the technique to the success of *Pride and Prejudice*. As A. Walton Litz puts it (see page 59 below), it gives the reader "a sense of involvement and identification while simultaneously providing the perspective necessary for moral judgment." More specifically, it puts the reader in a moral position at once committed and disengaged with respect to the difficulties and weaknesses of the heroine—bound to Elizabeth in her confusions and errors, yet amused and fascinated by the stubborn fidelity to her own original opinions which so complicates her struggles. Particularly when seen in light of the history of the English novel, in the context both of the models available to the author and of later nineteenth- and twentieth-century developments in novelistic technique, the method of *Pride and Prejudice* appears nothing short of a triumph.

But the purely novelistic elements in the composition of the novel cannot alone explain its success and popularity. Long before one has succeeded in analyzing its narrative strategies, one has been caught up in its seductive comic spirit and perhaps remarked its strong affinities with stage comedy. It is no accident that, of Jane Austen's

---

[8] *The Rise of the Novel*, p. 297.

six novels, *Pride and Prejudice* is still, as far as I can ascertain, the only one to have been redone more than once for stage representation. It is certainly the only one to have been transformed into a major Hollywood movie. It has even turned up, albeit unsuccessfully, under its original title of *First Impressions* as a Broadway musical. The essential theatricality of *Pride and Prejudice,* to which all these transformations testify, is evident first of all in the very shape of the book: as Mr. Litz remarks on page 68, the "tripartite structure of *Pride and Prejudice,* dictated by the conventional three-decker form of publication, is similar to the structure of a three-act play." And this observation is worth developing in directions other than those Mr. Litz himself has elected to follow. If we wish to situate the novel accurately in the context of English literary history, we must look beyond novelistic considerations, for the pacing, the wit, the essential tone of the book are at least as closely connected to certain classic stage comedies as to the work of any other English novelist.

It should be noted first that the links between the old genre of comedy and the newer one of the novel are in general quite close. If one thinks of the novel's definitive reluctance to participate in the high-flown language of epic and tragedy, of its preoccupation with figures below the highest stations of life, and of its frequent concern with the difficulties of lovers and its characteristic resolution in marriage, one begins to see the novel, however uncomic in some of its particular manifestations, as an offspring of the tradition of comedy. In the case of *Pride and Prejudice* there exists a still closer resemblance. Its many scenes of elegantly balanced repartee point backward in time toward Congreve and the comedy of manners. But other essential elements point still further backward toward the romantic comedies of Shakespeare.

In *Pride and Prejudice,* as in the typical romantic comedy of Shakespeare, we find the uneasy and uncertain wooings, elaborate formal balancing of characters around the themes of love, final revelations, reconciliations, and irresistible happy ending; above all, we find an engaging young woman whose audacity and brightness make things happen yet who must learn to see herself the temporary victim of her own inventions, and who, in the end, willingly submits her cleverness to the higher claims of love. To be more specific, compare *Pride and Prejudice* with *Twelfth Night.* In each case, our sympathy toward the heroine is established at the outset, as Viola tries to find her way alone in a strange land and Elizabeth tries to find hers in a hostile world where selfishness begins at home. In each case, sympathy is qualified by our awareness that the heroine's self-confidence would only be appropriate in a world far simpler than the one we actually see and far less subject to the vagaries of love. Indeed, each work is kept going by the ironic reversals attendant upon the major characters' assumption of roles inappropriate to the prescribed conclusion, that conclusion being the resolution of all personal difficulties in marriage. Hence Viola's masculine disguise and the Duke's sybaritic effeteness and Olivia's election of endless asexual mourning are as subject to correction as Elizabeth's aggressive self-reliance and Darcy's social rigidity and the reluctance of Jane and Bingley to act in a clear and forthright manner upon the impulses of affection. Similarly, in both works certain secondary figures unavailable for meaningful marriage—Malvolio and Sir Andrew Aguecheek, Mr. Collins and Mary Bennet—provide the comic gloss upon the chosen few who, in that glow of delight and accommodation that bathes the conclusion of both works, have not only discovered themselves but at the same time affirmed the humane possibilities of social existence by facing up to their love. There are palpable differences between a *Twelfth Night* and a *Pride and Prejudice,* of course. The realistic conventions at work in the latter, for example, make possible a Charlotte Lucas while denying us a Sir Toby Belch, and Illyria is far from Pemberley or Longbourn. But the correspondences seem, in regard to overall effect upon the reader, more worthy of consideration than the differences, especially since both works have somewhere very near their center the dream of possible fulfillment in love which finds expression equally in the most guileless fairy tales, the glossiest Hollywood romances, and the subtlest masterworks of romantic comedy.

Not that the ending of *Pride and Prejudice* encourages the reader to put disorder and disappointment and obduracy out of his mind. The last paragraphs of the book recall to us that there are those like Mrs. Bennet who can never really be changed, that Lydias and Wickhams are forever stuck with one another, and so on. And here as everywhere in the novel, the pervasive irony—not only the narrator's irony but Elizabeth's own, which does not desert her even when she finds herself the châtelaine of a very great estate—brings us back again and again to the unalterable incongruities of life itself. Still, romantic comedy is animated by a spirit of forgiveness which, in Jane Austen's novel, operates perfectly against the toughness of the irony. Think of the scene near the end in which Mr. Bennet, appalled at the notion that his favorite daughter might be marrying only for advantage, reminds her of the results of incompatibility in marriage in a voice that passes from its wonted ironical cadences to an unexpected directness of expression:

> "Lizzy," said her father, "I have given him my consent. He is the kind of man, indeed, to whom I should never dare refuse any thing, which

he condescended to ask. I now give it to *you*, if you are resolved on having him. But let me advise you to think better of it. I know your disposition, Lizzy. I know that you could be neither happy nor respectable, unless you truly esteemed your husband; unless you looked up to him as a superior. Your lively talents would place you in the greatest danger in an unequal marriage. You could scarcely escape discredit and misery. My child, let me not have the grief of seeing *you* unable to respect your partner in life. You know not what you are about." (III, xvii)

Informed by Mr. Bennet's love for Elizabeth and his unique first-hand knowledge of what the "misery" of "an unequal marriage" actually consists of, this speech proclaims those simple and vulnerable human affections which, when thwarted, necessitate the mask of irony in the first place; it locates the theatrically conventional happy ending of the novel in a world in which sadness and loneliness may well serve as the norm. Or consider the description of Elizabeth's arrival at the Gardiners':

As they drove to Mr. Gardiner's door, Jane was at a drawing-room window watching their arrival; when they entered the passage she was there to welcome them, and Elizabeth, looking earnestly in her face, was pleased to see it healthful and lovely as ever. On the stairs were a troop of little boys and girls, whose eagerness for their cousin's appearance would not allow them to wait in the drawing-room, and whose shyness, as they had not seen her for a twelvemonth, prevented their coming lower. All was joy and kindness. (II, iv)

"All was joy and kindness": the phrase, out of context, could sound hopelessly sentimental, but the irony of the narrator's general style encourages us to accept without question any such rare expression of harmony. Jane Austen did not have at her disposal the poetry of Shakespeare or the music of Mozart, but she had her own way of pointing to the human foundation on which all her brilliant artifices are constructed.

As I have suggested, the spirit which *Pride and Prejudice* shares with a work like *Twelfth Night* (or a work like Mozart's *Figaro* or *Cosi Fan Tutte*) is likely to assert itself in the reader's experience long before any curiosity about the technical procedures of the book. That spirit, I believe, accounts in large measure for the extent to which the name of Jane Austen is popularly identified with *Pride and Prejudice*. Critics who know her writings well are likely to think *Emma* her most dazzling achievement, and in recent years the once-maligned *Mansfield Park* has inspired a remarkable amount of attention. But none of Jane Austen's other novels opens up as immediately and as directly as *Pride and Prejudice* the essential Austenian perspective, in part because none accepts so freely the congenial and wholly appropriate assumptions of romantic comedy.

IV. Pride and Prejudice *and the Critics*

Oddly enough, it may be qualities that the modern reader particularly admires in *Pride and Prejudice* that kept it from enjoying the wide recognition in its own century that it has found in ours. Not that Jane Austen lacked admirers from the beginning, and distinguished ones. The list includes Scott and Sheridan and Southey in her own lifetime, Macauley and George Henry Lewes and Tennyson in the next generation (all three of whom, with appropriate qualifications, compared her skills to Shakespeare's). As a rule, even those who disapproved of her—like Carlyle and Charlotte Brontë (who may later have recanted), Emerson and Mark Twain—at least did her the justice of attacking her with a vigor commensurate with her talent. In her love of pattern and design, in her determination to be satisfied with man as a social animal—qualities nowhere more clearly exemplified than in *Pride and Prejudice*—she may have seemed somewhat alien to the reading public of the late-Romantic and the Victorian ages. Whatever the cause, it would appear that, as far as most nineteenth-century readers were concerned, her books were to be placed on that shelf of polite classics that one did not have to feel guilty about not opening.

Even in the twentieth century, when Jane Austen's reputation began to swell, her work remained for many years untouched by the kind of critical examination it has more recently provoked. From the "Janeites" one could naturally expect nothing; that curious cult of idolators was (and is—the strain is by no means extinct) content to stare vapidly at the pages of her novels, cooing over "dear Jane" and sighing for the quaint carefree times in which she lived. But even those from whom more serious criticism could be anticipated in fact produced very little. Studies by A. C. Bradley[9] and Reginald Farrer[10] and the fine essay in appreciation by Virginia Woolf are among the few useful critical documents of the period prior to the onset of World War II. Yet in retrospect, this period may prove the single crucial one for those to whom Jane Austen's novels have meaning, for it was at this time—from the early 1920s onward—that the distinguished Oxonian, R. W. Chapman, labored to make Jane

---

[9] "Jane Austen," *Essays and Studies by Members of the English Association,* II (1911), 7–36.
[10] "Jane Austen," *Quarterly Review,* CCXXVII (1917), 1–30.

Austen's work at last fully available to the public. Not only did he bring to light and publish all the extant letters and biographical documents, and all the juvenilia and occasional writings and unfinished pieces as well; he also produced the definitive edition of the novels themselves, abundant in scholarly apparatus and lavish in its reproduction of materials from Jane Austen's own time and place. One is free to wonder whether it is entirely a matter of coincidence that significant criticism of Jane Austen began to occur in quantity only after Chapman had shown how much labor Jane Austen was worth.

At any rate, the first book-length study of Jane Austen to which the term "criticism" could seriously be applied appeared in 1939: Mary Lascelles' *Jane Austen and Her Art*. It is more than a little surprising to reread now its apologetic opening sentence: "I suppose that it must happen to writers on every one of the most generally interesting subjects of literary criticism to be told very often in the course of their writing that everything worth saying on that subject has been said already." On the other hand, she goes on, "it is likely that they may all feel (as I do) . . . that all who have written before them have stopped short as they were arriving at the most interesting point," [11] and in her own analyses (see, for example, pages 70–77 in this volume) Miss Lascelles quickly demonstrated how very little "worth saying" on the subject of Jane Austen's novels had yet been said, how far short of "the most interesting point" most earlier critics had fallen, and how much attention the subject could actually bear. At about the same time as Miss Lascelles' book, valuable essays on Jane Austen—"essays in iconoclasm" the somewhat conservative Mr. Chapman labeled them[12]—began to appear in the influential journal *Scrutiny* (including the first version of the piece by Reuben A. Brower included in this volume). Modern criticism had begun to catch up with Jane Austen.

The present collection has been made from writings on *Pride and Prejudice* of the last thirty years. Each of the essays in the first section constitutes a preface to the novel as a whole from a different point of reference; each of those in the second section, which might be subtitled, after E. M. Forster, "Aspects of the Novel," explores one particular compositional feature of the book. Anyone reading through these essays will be impressed by the degree to which, through patient attention, criticism has been able to show how the novel is put together and how it gains its effects upon its audience. But if he begins

[11] Oxford: Clarendon Press, 1939, p. v.
[12] *Jane Austen: a Critical Bibliography*, 2nd ed. (Oxford: Clarendon Press, 1955), p. 52.

to feel that in all this formal criticism he is about to lose sight of the book itself, he can turn to the fine little parody that closes the selection. Meant, I suppose, to subvert the premises of anthropological criticism by applying those premises to a novel set in a world as far removed as possible from the realms of primitive gods, Douglas Bush's essay assumes a further function when read in a book like this one. It brings us back to the kind of irony that is the trademark of Jane Austen herself, back to the laughter that technical analysis threatens to drown out. Like any great comedy, *Pride and Prejudice* should ideally be (to beg a phrase of Falstaff) "not only witty in itself, but the cause that wit is in other men."

PART ONE

Interpretations

On *Pride and Prejudice*

by Dorothy Van Ghent

It is the frequent response of readers who are making their first acquaintance with Jane Austen that her subject matter is itself so limited—limited to the manners of a small section of English country gentry who apparently never have been worried about death or sex, hunger or war, guilt or God—that it can offer no contiguity with modern interests. This is a very real difficulty in an approach to an Austen novel, and we should not obscure it; for by taking it initially into consideration, we can begin to come closer to the actual toughness and subtlety of the Austen quality. The greatest novels have been great in range as well as in technical invention; they have explored human experience a good deal more widely and deeply than Jane Austen was able to explore it. It is wronging an Austen novel to expect of it what it makes no pretense to rival—the spiritual profundity of the very greatest novels. But if we expect artistic mastery of limited materials, we shall not be disappointed.

The exclusions and limitations are deliberate; they do not necessarily represent limitations of Jane Austen's personal experience. Though she led the life of a maiden gentlewoman, it was not actually a sheltered life—not sheltered, that is, from the apparition of a number of the harsher human difficulties. She was a member of a large family whose activities ramified in many directions, in a period when a cousin could be guillotined, when an aunt and uncle could be jailed for a year on a shopkeeper's petty falsification, and when the pregnancies and childbed mortalities of relatives and friends were kept up at a barnyard rate. Her letters show in her the ironical mentality and the eighteenth-century gusto that are the reverse of the puritanism and naïveté that might be associated with the maidenly life. What she excludes from her fictional material does not, then, reflect a personal obliviousness, but, rather, a critically developed knowledge of the character of her gift and a restriction of its exercise to the kind of subject matter which she could shape into most significance. When we begin to look upon these limitations, not as having the negative function of showing how much of human life Jane Austen left out, but as having, rather, the positive function of defining the form and meaning of the book, we begin also to understand that kind of value that can lie in artistic mastery over a restricted range. This "two inches of ivory" (the metaphor which she herself used to describe her work), though it may resemble the handle of a lady's fan when looked on scantly, is in substance an elephant's tusk; it is a savagely probing instrument as well as a masterpiece of refinement.

Time and space are small in *Pride and Prejudice*. Time is a few months completely on the surface of the present, with no abysses of past or future, no room for mystery; there is time only for a sufficiently complicated business of getting wived and husbanded and of adapting oneself to civilization and civilization to oneself. Space can be covered in a few hours of coach ride between London and a country village or estate; but this space is a *physical* setting only in the most general-ized sense; it is space as defined by a modern positivistic philosopher —"a place for an argument." The concern is rational and social. What is relevant is the way minds operate in certain social circumstances, and the physical particular has only a derived and subordinate rel-evance, as it serves to stimulate attitudes between persons. Even the social circumstances are severely restricted: they are the circumstances of marriageable young women coming five to a leisure-class family with reduced funds and prospects. What can be done with this time and space and these circumstances? What Jane Austen does is to dissect—with what one critic has called "regulated hatred" [1]—the monster in the skin of the civilized animal, the irrational acting in the costumes and on the stage of the rational; and to illuminate the difficult and delicate reconciliation of the sensitively developed individual with the terms of his social existence.

"It is a truth universally acknowledged, that a single man in possession of a good fortune must be in want of a wife." This is the first sentence of the book. What we read in it is its opposite—a single woman must be in want of a man with a good fortune—and at once we are inducted into the Austen language, the ironical Austen attack, and the energy, peculiar to an Austen novel, that arises from the compression between a barbaric subsurface marital warfare and a

---

[1] D. W. Harding, "Regulated Hatred: An Aspect of the Work of Jane Austen," *Scrutiny*, March, 1940.

surface of polite manners and civilized conventions. Marriage—that adult initiatory rite that is centrally important in most societies whether barbarous or advanced—is the uppermost concern. As motivation for the story, it is as primitively powerful an urgency as is sex in a novel by D. H. Lawrence. The tale is that of a man hunt, with the female the pursuer and the male a shy and elusive prey. The desperation of the hunt is the desperation of economic survival: girls in a family like that of the Bennets must succeed in running down solvent young men in order to survive. But the marriage motivation is complicated by other needs of a civilized community: the man hunters must observe the most refined behavior and sentiments. The female is a "lady" and the male is a "gentleman"; they must "fall in love." Not only must civilized appearances be preserved before the eyes of the community, but it is even necessary to preserve dignity and fineness of feeling in one's own eyes.

The second sentence outlines the area in which the aforementioned "truth universally acknowledged" is to be investigated—a small settled community, febrile with social and economic rivalry.

> However little known the feelings or views of such a man may be on his first entering a neighborhood, this truth is so well fixed in the minds of the surrounding families, that he is considered as the rightful property of some one or other of their daughters.

Here a high valuation of property is so dominant a culture trait that the word "property" becomes a metaphor for the young man himself; and the phrasing of the sentence, with typical Austen obliquity, adds a further sly emphasis to this trait when it uses an idiom associated with the possession of wealth—"well fixed"—as a qualifier of the standing of "truth." We are told that the young man may have "feelings or views" of his own (it becomes evident, later, that even daughters are capable of a similar willful subjectivity); and we are warned of the embarrassment such "feelings or views" will cause, whether to the individual or to the community, when we read of those "surrounding families" in whom "truth" is "so well fixed"— portentous pressure! And now we are given a light preliminary draft of the esteemed state of marriage, in the little drama of conflicting perceptions and wills that the first chapter presents between the imbecilic Mrs. Bennet and her indifferent, sarcastic husband. "The experience of three and twenty years had been insufficient to make his wife understand his character." The marriage problem is set broadly before us in this uneasy parental background, where an ill-mated couple must come to terms on the finding of mates for their five daughters. A social call must be made, in any case, on the single

gentleman of good fortune who has settled in the neighborhood. With
the return of the call, and with the daughters set up for view—some of
whom are "handsome," some "good-natured"—no doubt he will buy,
that is to say, "fall in love" (with such love, perhaps, as we have seen
between Mr. and Mrs. Bennet themselves).

In this first chapter, the fundamental literary unit of the single
word—"fortune," "property," "possession," "establishment," "business"
—has consistently been setting up the impulsion of economic interest
against those non-utilitarian interests implied by the words "feelings"
and "love." [2] The implications of the word "marriage" itself are ambivalent; for as these implications are controlled in the book, "marriage"
does not mean an act of ungoverned passion (not even in Lydia's and
Wickham's rash elopement does it mean this: for Wickham has his
eye on a settlement by blackmail, and Lydia's infatuation is rather
more with a uniform than with a man); marriage means a complex
engagement between the marrying couple and society—that is, it
means not only "feelings" but "property" as well. In marrying, the
individual marries society as well as his mate, and "property" provides
the necessary articles of this other marriage. With marriage, so defined,
as the given locus of action, the clash and reconciliation of utility
interests with interests that are nonutilitarian will provide a subtle
drama of manners; for whatever spiritual creativity may lie in the
individual personality, that creativity will be able to operate only
within publicly acceptable modes of deportment. These modes of
deportment, however public and traditional, must be made to convey
the secret life of the individual spirit, much as a lens conveys a vision
of otherwise invisible constellations. Language itself is the lens in this
case—the linguistic habits of social man.

Below language we do not descend, except by inference, for, in this
definitively social world, language is the index of behavior, the special
machine which social man has made to register his attitudes and to
organize his dealings with others. We have spoken of Jane Austen's
exclusion of the physical particular. One might expect that in her
treatment of the central problem of marriage she could not avoid some
physical particularity—some consciousness of the part played by the
flesh and the fleshly passions in marriage. Curiously and quite wonderfully, out of her restricted concern for the rational and social definition
of the human performance there does arise a strong implication of the
physical. Can one leave this novel without an acute sense of physical
characterizations—even of the smells of cosmetic tinctures and obesity
in Mrs. Bennet's boudoir, or of the grampus-like erotic wallowings of

---

[2] This point of view is developed by Mark Schorer in the essay "Fiction and the
'Analogical Matrix,'" in *Critiques and Essays on Modern Fiction*, edited by John
W. Aldridge (New York: The Ronald Press Company, 1952), pp. 83–98.

the monstrous Mr. Collins? Nothing could be stranger to an Austen novel than such representations of the physical. And yet, from her cool, unencumbered understanding of the linguistic exhibitions of the parlor human, she gives us, by the subtlest of implication, the human down to its "naturals," down to where it is human only by grace of the fact that it talks English and has a set of gestures arbitrarily corresponding to rationality.

Among the "daughters" and the "young men of fortune" there are a few sensitive individuals, civilized in spirit as well as in manner. For these few, "feeling" must either succumb to the paralysis of utility or else must develop special delicacy and strength. The final adjustment with society, with "property" and "establishment," must be made in any case, for in this book the individual is unthinkable without the social environment, and in the Austen world that environment has been given once and forever—it is unchangeable and it contains the only possibilities for individual development. For the protagonists, the marriage rite will signify an "ordeal" in that traditional sense of a moral testing which is the serious meaning of initiation in any of the important ceremonies of life. What will be tested will be their integrity of "feeling" under the crudely threatening social pressures. The moral life, then, will be equated with delicacy and integrity of feeling, and its capacity for growth under adverse conditions. In the person of the chief protagonist, Elizabeth, it really will be equated with intelligence. In this conception of the moral life, Jane Austen shows herself the closest kin to Henry James in the tradition of the English novel; for by James, also, the moral life was located in emotional intelligence, and he too limited himself to observation of its workings in the narrow area of a sophisticated civilization.

The final note of the civilized in *Pride and Prejudice* is, as we have said, reconciliation. The protagonists do not "find themselves" by leaving society, divorcing themselves from its predilections and obsessions. In the union of Darcy and Elizabeth, Jane and Bingley, the obsessive social formula of marriage-to-property is found again, but now as the happy reward of initiates who have travailed and passed their "ordeal." The incongruities between savage impulsions and the civilized conventions in which they are buried, between utility and morality, are reconciled in the symbolic act of a marriage which society itself—bent on useful marriages—has paradoxically done everything to prevent. Rightly, the next to the last word in the book is the word "uniting."

We have so far attempted to indicate both the restrictive discipline which Jane Austen accepted from her material and the moral life which she found in it. The significance of a given body of material is a function of the form which the artist gives to the material. Significance

is, then, not actually "found" by the artist in his subject matter, as
if it were already and obviously present there for anyone to see, but
is created by him in the act of giving form to the material (it was in
this sense that poets were once called trouvères, or "finders"). The
form of the action of *Pride and Prejudice* is a set of "diverging and
converging lines" [3] mathematically balanced in their movements, a
form whose diagrammatic neatness might be suggested in such a design
as that given below, which shows the relationship of correspondence-

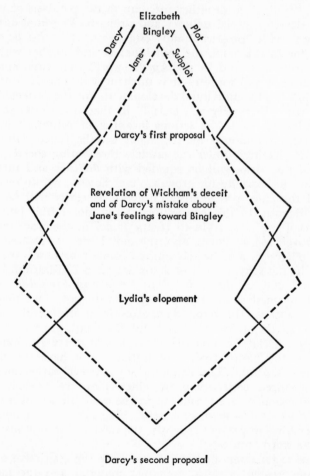

Elizabeth

Bingley

Darcy

Jane

Plot

Subplot

Darcy's first proposal

Revelation of Wickham's deceit
and of Darcy's mistake about
Jane's feelings toward Bingley

Lydia's elopement

Darcy's second proposal

[3] The phrase and the observation are those of Mary Lascelles, in *Jane Austen
and Her Art* (New York: Oxford University Press, 1939), p. 160.

with-variation between the Darcy-Elizabeth plot and the Jane-Bingley subplot, the complication of the former and the simplicity of the latter, the successive movements toward splitting apart and toward coming together, and the final resolution of movement in "recognition" and reconciliation between conflicting claims, as the total action composes itself in the shape of the lozenge. . . .

But significant form, as we have noted in previous studies, is a far more complex structure of relationships than those merely of plot. An Austen novel offers a particularly luminous illustration of the function of style in determining the major form. Our diagram of the plot movements of *Pride and Prejudice* will serve as visualization of a pattern of antithetical balances found also in the verbal composition of the book. It is here, in style, in the language base itself, that we are able to observe Jane Austen's most deft and subtle exploitation of her material.

The first sentence of the book—"It is a truth universally acknowledged, that a single man in possession of a good fortune must be in want of a wife"—again affords an instance in point. As we have said, the sentence ironically turns itself inside out, thus: a single woman must be in want of a man with a good fortune. In this doubling of the inverse meaning over the surface meaning, a very modest-looking statement sums up the chief conflicting forces in the book: a decorous convention of love (which holds the man to be the pursuer) embraces a savage economic compulsion (the compulsion of the insolvent female to run down male "property"), and in the verbal embrace they appear as a unit. The ironic mode here is a mode of simultaneous opposition and union: civilized convention and economic primitivism unite in the sentence as they do in the action, where "feelings" and "fortune," initially in conflict, are reconciled in the socially creative union of marriage.

This is but one type of verbal manipulation with which the book luxuriates. Another we shall illustrate with a sentence from Mr. Collins' proposal to Elizabeth, where "significant form" lies in elaborate rather than in modest phrasing. Mr. Collins manages to wind himself up almost inextricably in syntax.

> "But the fact is, that being as I am, to inherit this estate after the death of your honored father, (who, however, may live many years longer,) I could not satisfy myself without resolving to chuse a wife from among his daughters, that the loss to them might be as little as possible, when the melancholy event takes place—which, however, as I have already said, may not be for several years."

Fancy syntax acts here, not as an expression of moral and intellectual refinement (as Mr. Collins intends it to act), but as an expression of

stupidity, the antithesis of that refinement. The elaborate language in
which Mr. Collins gets himself fairly *stuck* is a mimesis of an action
of the soul, the soul that becomes self dishonest through failure to
know itself, and that overrates itself at the expense of the social
context, just as it overrates verbalism at the expense of meaning. We
have suggested that moral life, in an Austen novel, is identified with
emotional intelligence; and it is precisely through failure of intelligence—the wit to know his own limitations—that Mr. Collins appears
as a moral monstrosity. Language is the mirror of his degeneracy.
Against Mr. Collins' elaborate style of speech we may place the neat
and direct phrasing of a sentence such as "It is a truth universally
acknowledged . . ." where the balance of overt thesis and buried
antithesis acts as a kind of signature of the intelligential life—its
syntactical modesty conveying a very deft and energetic mental dance.

Similarly, elaborate epithet ("your honored father," "the melancholy
event") is suspect—the sign not of attention but of indifference, of a
moldiness of spirit which, far from being innocuous, has the capacity
of mold to flourish destructively and to engulf what is clean and sound,
as such epithet itself devours sense. Comedy, let us say again, "is a
serious matter," and what is serious in this scene of Mr. Collins'
proposal is the engulfing capacity of the rapacious Mr. Collins, from
whom Elizabeth escapes narrowly. The narrowness of the escape is
underlined by the fact that Elizabeth's friend, Charlotte—herself, we
assume, intelligent, inasmuch as she is Elizabeth's friend—compla-
cently offers herself as host to this mighty mold. In the civilized
community which is our area of observation, emotional intelligence
and quickness of moral perception—as we see them, for instance, in
Elizabeth—are profoundly threatened by an all-environing imbecility.
It is through style that we understand the nature of this threat; for
the simplicity and directness of the governing syntax of the book
prepares us to find positive values in simplicity and directness, negative values in elaboration and indirection. Even the canny intelligence
of Mr. Bennet is not that emotionally informed intelligence—or, shall
we say, that intelligence which informs the emotions—that we are
led to look upon as desirable; and Mr. Bennet reveals his failure also
in "style," a style of speech that shows a little too elaborate consciousness of the pungency of double-talk, of the verbal effect of ironic
undercutting. When Elizabeth suggests that it would be imprudent to
send the lightheaded Lydia to Brighton, he says,

Lydia will never be easy till she has exposed herself in some public
place or other, and we can never expect her to do it with so little expense
or inconvenience to her family as under the present circumstances.

Being intelligent, Mr. Bennet learns regret for his failure, although (and we delight also in Jane Austen's "realism" here, the tenacity of her psychological grip on her characters) not too much regret—not so much that he ceases to be Mr. Bennet.

From still another point of view, the style of the book is significant of total structure; we refer here to a generalized kind of epithet used in descriptive passages. The park at Pemberley, Darcy's estate, "was very large, and contained great variety of ground"; one drove "through a beautiful wood stretching over a wide extent." What we wish to notice, in diction of this kind, is the merely approximate appropriateness of the qualifier: "large," "great variety," "beautiful wood," "wide extent." This type of diction we might again describe as "modest," or we might speak of it as flatly commonplace; but we shall want to investigate its possibilities of function in the total form of the book. The reader will observe the continued use of the same kind of diction in the passage below, describing the house; what should be noted is the use to which the description is put—its use, not to convey any sense of "naturalistic" particularity, but, rather, to reveal Darcy's taste (of which Elizabeth has been suspicious) and a subtle turn in Elizabeth's feelings about him.

> It was a large, handsome, stone building, standing well on rising ground, and backed by a ridge of high woody hills;—and in front, a stream of some natural importance was swelled into greater, but without any artificial appearance. Its banks were neither formal nor falsely adorned. Elizabeth was delighted. She had never seen a place for which nature had done more, or where natural beauty had been so little counteracted by an awkward taste. They were all of them warm in their admiration; and at that moment she felt that to be mistress of Pemberley might be something!

Wealth applied to the happiest and most dignified creation of environment—that is all we need to know about this setting, a need which the description fulfills by virtue of generalizations—"large," "standing well," "natural importance," "natural beauty," and the series of negations of what is generally understood by "artificial appearance," "falsely adorned," and so forth. More particularity of description would deflect from what is significant in the episode, namely, the effect of the scene upon Elizabeth's attitude toward her lover. Darcy himself has had in her eyes a certain artificiality, unpleasant formality, falseness; he has been lacking in that naturalness which delights her in the present scene, which is his home and which speaks intimately of him; and she has felt that his taste in the handling of human relations was very seriously "awkward." The appearance of

Pemberley cannot help putting a slight pressure on her judgment of him, and the description is used with deliberate purpose for this effect. And how shrewd psychologically and warmly human is the remark, "and at that moment she felt that to be mistress of Pemberley might be something!" With all her personal integrity and exacerbated delicacy of feeling about the horrors of acquisitiveness, Elizabeth is smitten with an acquisitive temptation. (No wonder Jane Austen could not find Elizabeth's painted portrait in the galleries, though she was able to find Jane Bennet's there. Elizabeth is quite too human to have a duplicate in paint; only language is able to catch her.) In this final clause, the dramatic concern is solely with the social context—the shifting attitudes of one person toward another, as these attitudes are conditioned by the terms of a narrow, but nevertheless complex, social existence; but as the relationships between persons shift, the individual himself (as Elizabeth, here) is reinterpreted, shows a new aspect of his humanity. In this fashion, the Austen style—here a deliberately generalized and commonplace descriptive style—functions again as determination of significant form, significance in this particular case being the *rational* meaning of a physical setting.

Finally we should remark upon what is perhaps the most formative and conclusive activity of style in the book: the effect of a narrowly mercantile and materialistic vocabulary in setting up meanings. Let us go down a few lists of typical words, categorizing them rather crudely and arbitrarily, but in such a manner as to show their direction of reference.[4] The reader will perhaps be interested in adding to these merely suggestive lists, for in watching the Austen language lies the real excitement of the Austen novel. We shall set up such categories as "trade," "arithmetic," "money," "material possessions," simply in order to indicate the kind of language Jane Austen inherited from her culture and to which she was confined—and in order to suggest what she was able to do with her language, how much of the human drama she was able to get into such confines.

We could add such verbal categories as those referring to "patronage," "law," "skill" (a particularly interesting one, covering such words as "design," "cunning," "arts," "schemes," and so on; a category obviously converging with the "trade" category, but whose vocabulary, as it appears in this book, is used derogatorily—the stupid people, like Mrs. Bennet, Lady Catherine de Bourgh, Wickham, and Mr. Collins, are the ones who "scheme" and have "designs").

In viewing in the abstract the expressive possibilities open to literary creatorship, we might assume that the whole body of the English

---

[4] Mr. Schorer's essay "Fiction and the 'Analogical Matrix,'" cited above, closely examines this aspect of Jane Austen's style.

Trade	Arithmetic	Money	Material Possessions	Social Integration
employed	equally	pounds	estate	town
due form	added	credit	property	society
collect	proportion	capital	owner	civil
receipt	addition	pay	house	neighborhood
buy	enumerate	fortune	manor	county
sell	figure	valuable	tenant	fashion
business	calculated	principal	substantial	breeding
supply	amount	interest	establishment	genteel
terms	amounting	afford	provided	marriage
means	inconsiderable	indebted	foundation	husband
venture	consideration	undervalue	belongs to	connection

language, as it is filed in the dictionary, is perfectly free of access to
each author—that each author shares equally and at large in the
common stuff of the language. In a sense this is true; the whole body of
the language *is* there, virtually, in the dictionary, and anyone can
consult it and use it if he wants to. But we have observed fairly frequently, if only by-the-way, in these studies, that each author does not
consult the whole body of the language in selecting words for his
meanings; that he is driven, as if compulsively, to the selection of a
highly particular part of the language; and that the individual
character of his work, its connotations and special insights, derive
largely from the style he has made his own—that is to say, from
the vocabulary and verbal arrangements he has adopted out of the
whole gamut of words and rhetorical patterns available in the language. In making these selections, he is acting partly under the compulsions of the culture in which he has been bred and whose
unconscious assumptions—as to what is interesting or valuable or
necessary or convenient in life—are reflected in the verbal and
rhetorical selections common in that culture; and he is acting partly
also under compulsions that are individual to his own personal background, but that still maintain subtle links with the common cultural
assumptions. The general directions of reference taken by Jane
Austen's language, as indicated by such lists as those given above (and
the lists, with others like them, could be extended for pages), are
clearly materialistic. They reflect a culture whose institutions are
solidly defined by materialistic interests—property and banking and
trade and the law that keeps order in these matters—institutions
which determine, in turn, the character of family relations, the
amenities of community life, and the whole complex economy of the
emotions. By acknowledgment of the fact that the materialistic as-

sumptions of our own culture are even more pervasive than those
reflected in this book, and that their governance over our emotions
and our speech habits is even more grim, more sterilizing, and more
restrictive, we should be somewhat aided in appreciation of the "con-
temporaneity" of Jane Austen herself.

But where then, we must ask, does originality lie, if an author's
very language is dictated in so large a part by something, as it were,
"outside" himself—by the culture into which he is accidentally born?
How can there be any free play of individual genius, the free and
original play with the language by which we recognize the insight and
innovations of genius? The question has to be answered separately
for the work of each artist, but as for Jane Austen's work we have
been finding answers all along—in her exploitation of antithetical
structures to convey ambivalent attitudes, in her ironic use of syntactical elaborations that go against the grain of the language and that
convey moral aberrations, and finally in her direct and oblique play
with an inherited vocabulary that is materialistic in reference and that
she forces—or blandishes or intrigues—into spiritual duties.

The language base of the Austen novel gives us the limiting conditions of the culture. Somehow, using this language of acquisitiveness
and calculation and materialism, a language common to the most
admirable characters as well as to the basest characters in the book,
the spiritually creative persons will have to form their destinies.
The project would be so much easier if the intelligent people and
the stupid people, the people who are morally alive and the people
who are morally dead, had each their different language to distinguish
and publicize their differences! But unfortunately for that ease, they
have only one language. Fortunately for the drama of the Austen
novel, there is this difficulty of the single materialistic language; for
drama subsists on difficulty. Within the sterile confines of public
assumptions, the Austen protagonists find with difficulty the fertility
of honest and intelligent individual feeling. On a basis of communica-
tion that is drawn always from the public and savage theology of
"property," the delicate lines of spiritual adjustment are explored.
The final fought-for recognitions of value are recognitions of the unity
of experience—a unity between the common culture and the individual development. No one more knowledgeably than this perceptive and witty woman, ambushed by imbecility, could have
conducted such an exploration.

Light and Bright and Sparkling:
Irony and Fiction in *Pride and Prejudice*

by Reuben A. Brower

The work is rather too light, and bright, and sparkling; it wants shade;
it wants to be stretched out here and there with a long chapter of
sense, if it could be had; if not, of solemn specious nonsense. . . .

JANE AUSTEN

Many pages of *Pride and Prejudice* can be read as sheer poetry of
wit, as Pope without couplets. The antitheses are almost as frequent
and almost as varied; the play of ambiguities is certainly as complex;
the orchestration of tones is as precise and subtle. As in the best of
Pope, the displays of ironic wit are not without imaginative connection; what looks most diverse is really most similar, and ironies are
linked by vibrant reference to basic certainties. There are passages
too in which the rhythmical pattern of the sentence approaches the
formal balance of the heroic couplet:

> Mr. Bennet was so odd a mixture of quick parts, sarcastic humour,
> reserve, and caprice, that the experience of three and twenty years had
> been insufficient to make his wife understand his character. *Her* mind
> was less difficult to develope. She was a woman of mean understanding,
> little information, and uncertain temper. When she was discontented she
> fancied herself nervous. The business of her life was to get her daughters
> married; its solace was visiting and news.

The triumph of the novel—whatever its limitations may be—lies
in combining such poetry of wit with the dramatic structure of fiction.
In historical terms, to combine the traditions of poetic satire with

those of the sentimental novel, that was Jane Austen's feat in *Pride and Prejudice*.

For the "bright and sparkling," seemingly centrifugal play of irony is dramatically functional. It makes sense as literary art, the sense with which a writer is most concerned. The repartee, while constantly amusing, delineates characters and their changing relations and points the way to a climactic moment in which the change is most clearly recognized. Strictly speaking, this union of wit and drama is achieved with complete success only in the central sequence of *Pride and Prejudice*, in the presentation of Elizabeth's and Darcy's gradual revaluation of each other. Here, if anywhere, Jane Austen met James's demand that the novel should give its readers the maximum of "fun"; at the same time she satisfied the further standard implied in James's remark that the art of the novel is "above all an art of preparations." That she met these demands more continuously in *Emma* does not detract from her achievement in *Pride and Prejudice*.

Her blend of ironic wit and drama may be seen in its simplest form in the first chapter of the novel, in the dialogue between Mr. and Mrs. Bennet on the topic of Mr. Bingley's leasing Netherfield Park. Every remark which each makes, Mrs. Bennet petulantly, and Mr. Bennet perversely, bounces off the magnificent opening sentence:

> It is a truth universally acknowledged, that a single man in possession of a good fortune, must be in want of a wife.

The scene that follows dramatizes the alternatives implied in "universally," Mrs. Bennet reminding us of one; and Mr. Bennet, of the other:

> "My dear Mr. Bennet," said his lady to him one day, "have you heard that Netherfield Park is let at last?"
>
> Mr. Bennet replied that he had not.
>
> "But it is," returned she; "for Mrs. Long has just been here, and she told me all about it."
>
> Mr. Bennet made no answer.
>
> "Do not you want to know who has taken it?" cried his wife impatiently.
>
> "*You* want to tell me, and I have no objection to hearing it."
>
> This was invitation enough.
>
> "Why, my dear, you must know, Mrs. Long says that Netherfield is taken by a young man of large fortune from the north of England; that he came down on Monday in a chaise and four to see the place, and was so much delighted with it that he agreed with Mr. Morris immediately; that he is to take possession before Michaelmas, and some of his servants are to be in the house by the end of next week."
>
> "What is his name?"
>
> "Bingley."

"Is he married or single?"

"Oh! single, my dear, to be sure! A single man of large fortune; four or five thousand a year. What a fine thing for our girls!"

"How so? how can it affect them?"

"My dear Mr. Bennet," replied his wife, "how can you be so tiresome! You must know that I am thinking of his marrying one of them."

"Is that his design in settling here?"

"Design! nonsense, how can you talk so!"

A parallel appears in the opening of Pope's Epistle, "Of the Characters of Women":

> Nothing so true as what you once let fall,
> "Most Women have no Characters at all,"

a pronouncement immediately followed by a series of portraits showing that women have "characters" in one sense if not in another. It is also easy to find counterparts in Pope's satirical mode for Mr. Bennet's extreme politeness of address, his innocent queries, and his epigrammatic turns. The character that emerges from this dialogue is almost that of a professional satirist: Mr. Bennet is a man of quick parts and sarcastic humor, altogether a most unnatural father. Mrs. Bennet speaks another language; *her* talk does not crackle with irony and epigram; *her* sentences run in quite another mold. They either go on too long or break up awkwardly in impulsive exclamations; this is the talk of a person of "mean understanding" and "uncertain temper."

But though the blended art of this scene is admirable, a limitation appears. Mr. and Mrs. Bennet are so perfectly done that little more is left to be expressed. Variety or forward movement in the drama will almost surely be difficult, which obviously proves to be the case. The sequences that depend most closely on the opening scene—those concerned with the business of getting the Bennet daughters married—are all amusingly ironic, but relatively static as drama. As Mrs. Bennet contrives to join Jane and Bingley, to marry one daughter to Mr. Collins, and to further Lydia's exploits with the military, father, mother, and daughters remain in very nearly the same dramatic positions. True enough, the last of these sequences ends in a catastrophe. But the connection between Lydia's downfall and the earlier scenes of ironic comedy in which Mr. and Mrs. Bennet are opposed is not fully expressed. Lydia's behavior "leads to this" in a Richardsonian moral sense, but Lydia is too scantly presented in relation to her parents or to Wickham to prepare us adequately for her bad end. We accept it if at all as literary convention. Incidentally, we might conjecture that the marriage-market sequences belong to the early version of *Pride and Prejudice,* or at least that they are examples of Jane Austen's earlier manner. In the central sequence of *Pride and Prejudice,* especially in its more complex blend of ironic and dramatic design, we can see anticipated the more mature structure of both *Mansfield Park* and *Emma.*

In portraying the gradual change in Elizabeth's estimate of Darcy and in his attitude to her, Jane Austen achieves a perfect harmony between the rich ambiguity of ironic dialogue and the movement toward the climactic scenes in which the new estimate is revealed. I shall limit my discussion to scenes from the Elizabeth-Darcy narrative through the episode in which Elizabeth recognizes her "change in sentiment." Let us first read Jane Austen's dialogue as poetry of wit, disregarding for the time being any forward movement in the drama, and observing the variety of the irony and the unity of effect achieved through recurrent patterns and through assumptions shared by writer and reader. As in our reading of Pope, we may in this way appreciate the extraordinary richness of ironic texture and the imaginative continuity running through the play of wit. In analyzing the ironies and the assumptions, we shall see how intensely dramatic the dialogue is, dramatic in the sense of defining characters through the way they speak and are spoken about.

The aura of implications which surrounds many of the dialogues between Elizabeth and Darcy is complex enough to delight the most pure Empsonian. Take for example the dialogue in which Sir William Lucas attempts to interest Mr. Darcy in dancing:

> . . . Elizabeth at that instant moving towards them, he was struck with the notion of doing a very gallant thing, and called out to her,
>
> "My dear Miss Eliza, why are not you dancing?—Mr. Darcy, you must allow me to present this young lady to you as a very desirable partner.— You cannot refuse to dance, I am sure, when so much beauty is before you." And taking her hand, he would have given it to Mr. Darcy, who, though extremely surprised, was not unwilling to receive it, when she instantly drew back, and said with some discomposure to Sir William,
>
> "Indeed, Sir, I have not the least intention of dancing.—I entreat you not to suppose that I moved this way in order to beg for a partner."
>
> Mr. Darcy with grave propriety requested to be allowed the honour of her hand; but in vain. Elizabeth was determined; nor did Sir William at all shake her purpose by his attempt at persuasion.
>
> "You excel so much in the dance, Miss Eliza, that it is cruel to deny me the happiness of seeing you; and though this gentleman dislikes the amusement in general, he can have no objection, I am sure, to oblige us for one half hour."
>
> "Mr. Darcy is all politeness," said Elizabeth, smiling.
>
> "He is indeed—but considering the inducement, my dear Miss Eliza,

we cannot wonder at his complaisance; for who would object to such a partner?"

Elizabeth looked archly, and turned away.

"Mr. Darcy is all politeness": the statement, as Elizabeth might say, has a "teazing" variety of meanings. Mr. Darcy is polite in the sense indicated by "grave propriety," that is, he shows the courtesy appropriate to a gentleman—which is the immediate, public meaning of Elizabeth's compliment. But "grave propriety," being a very limited form of politeness, reminds us forcibly of Mr. Darcy's earlier behavior. His "gravity" at the ball had been "forbidding and disagreeable." "Grave propriety" may also mean the bare civility of "the proudest, most disagreeable man in the world." So Elizabeth's compliment has an ironic twist: she smiles and looks "archly." "All politeness" has also quite another meaning. Mr. Darcy "was not unwilling to receive" her hand. He is polite in more than the public proper sense; his gesture shows that he is interested in Elizabeth as a person. Her archness and her smile have for the reader an added ironic value: Elizabeth's interpretation of Darcy's manner may be quite wrong. Finally, there is the embracing broadly comic irony of Sir William's action. "Struck with the notion of doing a very gallant thing," he is pleasantly unconscious of what he is in fact doing and of what Elizabeth's remark may mean to her and to Darcy.

A similar cluster of possibilities appears in another conversation in which Darcy asks Elizabeth to dance with him:

> . . . soon afterwards Mr. Darcy, drawing near Elizabeth, said to her—
>
> "Do not you feel a great inclination, Miss Bennet, to seize such an opportunity of dancing a reel?"
>
> She smiled, but made no answer. He repeated the question, with some surprise at her silence.
>
> "Oh!" said she, "I heard you before; but I could not immediately determine what to say in reply. You wanted me, I know, to say 'Yes,' that you might have the pleasure of despising my taste; but I always delight in overthrowing those kind of schemes, and cheating a person of their premeditated contempt. I have therefore made up my mind to tell you, that I do not want to dance a reel at all—and now despise me if you dare."
>
> "Indeed I do not dare."
>
> Elizabeth, having rather expected to affront him, was amazed at his gallantry; but there was a mixture of sweetness and archness in her manner which made it difficult for her to affront anybody; and Darcy had never been so bewitched by any woman as he was by her. He really believed, that were it not for the inferiority of her connections, he should be in some danger.
>
> Miss Bingley saw, or suspected enough to be jealous; and her great

anxiety for the recovery of her dear friend Jane, received some assistance
from her desire of getting rid of Elizabeth.

    She often tried to provoke Darcy into disliking her guest, by talking of
their supposed marriage, and planning his happiness in such an alliance.

Again Mr. Darcy's request may be interpreted more or less pleasantly,
depending on whether we connect it with his present or past behavior.
Again Elizabeth's attack on Darcy and her archness have an irony beyond the irony intended by the speaker. But the amusement of this
dialogue lies especially in the variety of possible tones which we de-
tect in Darcy's speeches. Elizabeth hears his question as expressing
"premeditated contempt" and scorn of her own taste. But from Mr.
Darcy's next remark and the comment which follows, and from his
repeating his question and showing "some surprise," we may hear in
his request a tone expressive of some interest, perhaps only gallantry,
perhaps, as Elizabeth later puts it "somewhat of a friendlier nature."
We could take his "Indeed I do not dare" as pure gallantry (Elizabeth's version) or as a sign of conventional "marriage intentions"
(Miss Bingley's interpretation), if it were not for the nice reservation,
"He really believed, that were it not for the inferiority of her connections, he should be in some danger." We must hear the remark
as spoken with this qualification. This simultaneity of tonal layers
can be matched only in the satire of Pope, where, as we have seen,
the reader feels the impossibility of adjusting his voice to the rapid
changes in tone and the difficulty of representing by a single sound
the several sounds he hears as equally appropriate and necessary.
Analysis such as I have been making shows clearly how arbitrary and
how thin any stage rendering of *Pride and Prejudice* must be. No
speaking voice could possibly represent the variety of tones conveyed
to the reader by such interplay of dialogue and comment.

    It would be easy enough to produce more of these dialogues, es-
pecially on the subject of music or dancing, each with its range of
crisply differentiated meanings. Similar patterns of irony recur many
times. Mr. Darcy makes his inquiries (polite or impolite), asking with
a smile (scornful or encouraging) questions that may be interpreted as
pompous and condescending or gallant and well-disposed. So Mr. Darcy
cross-examines Elizabeth in the scene in which their "superior dancing" gives such pleasure to Sir William:

    "What think you of books?" said he, smiling.
    "Books—Oh! no.—I am sure we never read the same, or not with the
same feelings."
    "I am sorry you think so; but if that be the case, there can at least be
no want of subject.—We may compare our different opinions."

"No—I cannot talk of books in a ball-room; my head is always full of something else."

"The *present* always occupies you in such scenes—does it?" said he, with a look of doubt.

When connected with a hint of Darcy's changing attitude, that "look of doubt," Elizabeth's arch comments take on the added ironic value we have noted in other conversations.

Earlier in this dialogue, Darcy and Elizabeth run through the same sort of question and answer gamut, and with very nearly the same ironic dissonances:

He smiled, and assured her that whatever she wished him to say should be said.

"Very well.—That reply will do for the present.—Perhaps by and bye I may observe that private balls are much pleasanter than public ones.— But *now* we may be silent."

"Do you talk by rule then, while you are dancing?"

"Sometimes. One must speak a little, you know. It would look odd to be entirely silent for half an hour together, and yet for the advantage of *some,* conversation ought to be so arranged as that they may have the trouble of saying as little as possible."

"Are you consulting your own feelings in the present case, or do you imagine that you are gratifying mine?"

"Both," replied Elizabeth archly; "for I have always seen a great similarity in the turn of our minds.—We are each of an unsocial, taciturn disposition, unwilling to speak, unless we expect to say something that will amaze the whole room, and be handed down to posterity with all the eclat of a proverb."

"This is no very striking resemblance of your own character, I am sure," said he.

When Darcy himself is being quizzed he frequently remarks on his own behavior in a way that may be sublimely smug or simply self-respecting, as for example in his comment on his behavior at the first of the Hertfordshire balls:

"I certainly have not the talent which some people possess," said Darcy, "of conversing easily with those I have never seen before. I cannot catch their tone of conversation, or appear interested in their concerns, as I often see done."

But these conversations are not simply sets of ironic meanings; they are in more than a trivial sense *jeux d'esprit,* the play of an adult mind. (The sophistication they imply is of a kind which, as John Jay Chapman once remarked, is Greek and French, rather than English.) The fun in Jane Austen's dialogue has a serious point; or rather,

the fun *is* the point. The small talk is the focus for her keen sense of
the variability of character, for her awareness of the possibility that
the same remark or action has very different meanings in different
relations. What most satisfies us in reading the dialogue in *Pride and
Prejudice* is Jane Austen's awareness that it is difficult to know any
complex person, that knowledge of a man like Darcy is an interpretation and a construction, not a simple absolute. Like the characters
of Proust, the chief persons in *Pride and Prejudice* are not the same
when projected through the conversation of different people. The
snobisme of Darcy's talk, like Swann's, is measured according to the
group he is with. Mr. Darcy is hardly recognizable as the same man
when he is described by Mr. Wickham, by his housekeeper, or Elizabeth, or Mr. Bingley.

But it is only the complex persons, the "intricate characters," that
require and merit interpretation, as Elizabeth points out in the pleasant conversation in which she tells Bingley that she "understands him
perfectly":

> "You begin to comprehend me, do you?" cried he, turning towards her.
> "Oh! yes,—I understand you perfectly."
> "I wish I might take this for a compliment; but to be so easily seen
> through I am afraid is pitiful."
> "That is as it happens. It does not necessarily follow that a deep, in-
> tricate character is more or less estimable than such a one as yours."
> "Lizzy," cried her mother, "remember where you are, and do not run
> on in the wild manner that you are suffered to do at home."
> "I did not know before," continued Bingley immediately, "that you
> were a studier of character. It must be an amusing study."
> "Yes; but intricate characters are the *most* amusing. They have at least
> that advantage."
> "The country," said Darcy, "can in general supply but few subjects for
> such a study. In a country neighbourhood you move in a very confined
> and unvarying society."
> "But people themselves alter so much, that there is something new to
> be observed in them for ever."

Elizabeth's remark with its ironic application to Darcy indicates the
interest that makes the book "go" and shows the type of awareness we
are analyzing. "Intricate characters are the *most* amusing," because
their behavior can be taken in so many ways, because they are not always the same people. The man we know today is a different man to-
morrow. Naturally, we infer, people will not be equally puzzling to
every judge. Mr. Bingley and Jane find Mr. Darcy a much less "teazing" man than Elizabeth does. It is only the Elizabeths, the adult
minds, who will observe something new in the "same" people.

Such are the main assumptions behind the irony of *Pride and Prejudice,* as they are expressed through conversation studies of Darcy's character. In marked contrast with the opening scene of the novel, there is in these dialogues no nondramatic statement of the ironist's position, a further sign that in shaping the Elizabeth-Darcy sequence Jane Austen was moving away from the modes of satire toward more purely dramatic techniques.

While Jane Austen's irony depends on a sense of variability and intricacy of character, her vision is not one of Proustian relativity. The sense of variability is balanced by a vigorous and positive belief. Elizabeth, in commenting on Charlotte Lucas' choice of Mr. Collins, expresses very emphatically this combination of skepticism and faith:

> "My dear Jane, Mr. Collins is a conceited, pompous, narrow-minded silly man; you know he is, as well as I do; and you must feel, as well as I do, that the woman who marries him, cannot have a proper way of thinking. You shall not defend her, though it is Charlotte Lucas. You shall not, for the sake of one individual, change the meaning of principle and integrity, nor endeavour to persuade yourself or me, that selfishness is prudence, and insensibility of danger, security for happiness."

Though as usual Elizabeth's affirmations have an ironic overtone for the reader, they express a belief that is implied throughout *Pride and Prejudice.* There are persons such as Mr. Collins and Mrs. Bennet and Lady Catherine, about whom there can be no disagreement among people who "have a proper way of thinking." These fixed characters make up a set of certainties against which more intricate exhibitions of pride and prejudice are measured. They are the "fools" which James says are almost indispensable for any piece of fiction. For Jane Austen there can be no doubt about the meaning of "principle and integrity" and similar terms of value. Right-thinking persons know what pride is and when to apply the term. In common with her contemporaries Jane Austen enjoys the belief that some interpretations of behavior are more reasonable than others. The climactic scene of the novel, in which Elizabeth arrives at a new view of Darcy, shows us what is meant by a more reasonable interpretation: it is a reasoned judgment of character reached through long experience and slow weighing of probabilities. The certainty is an achieved certainty.

So the local ironies in Jane Austen, as in Pope, are defined and given larger significance through assumptions shared by the writer and public. The trivial dialogues are constantly being illuminated by a fine sense of the complexity of human nature and by a steady belief in the possibility of making sound judgments. At the same time the playfulness is always serving for "the illustration of character." (The term is Elizabeth's, though in applying it to Darcy, she is as usual unaware of its aptness to her own behavior.) Both she and Darcy are "illustrated" by their ambiguous questions and answers and the alternate interpretations which are so deftly indicated: the poetry of wit in *Pride and Prejudice* is completely dramatic. Certainly nothing could be more dramatic than the assumptions we have been describing: they reflect the practical dramatist's interest in human beings and their behavior, his awareness that character is expressed by what men say and do. The assumption that more reasonable interpretations of conduct are attainable provides for the movement toward a decisive change in relationships at the climax of the novel. It also lays the ground for the resolution of ambiguities and the cancellation of irony at the same moment.

We can now appreciate how beautifully the ironies of the dialogue function in the curve of the main dramatic sequence. The conversations have been skilfully shaped to prepare us for Elizabeth's revised estimate of Darcy, for her recognition that Darcy regards her differently, and for her consequent "change of sentiment" toward him. The preparation for this climax is made mainly through the controlled use of ambiguity that we have been observing. Though we are always being led to make double interpretations, we are never in confusion about what the alternatives are. It is important also that in these ironic dialogues no comment is included that makes us take Darcy's behavior in only an unpleasant sense. When there is comment, it is mainly used to bring out the latent ambiguity without in any way resolving it. So in general the earlier Darcy scenes are left open in preparation for a fresh estimate of his character. The pleasanter interpretation of one of Darcy's or Elizabeth's remarks or of one of the author's comments allows for the later choice and for the consequent recognitions. The pleasanter possibility also gives in passing a hint of Darcy's changing attitude to Elizabeth. For instance, the more favorable meaning of Elizabeth's "Mr. Darcy is all politeness" or of the comment on his "grave propriety" points forward to Darcy's perfect courtesy at Pemberley and to Elizabeth's admission that he was right in objecting to her family's "impropriety of conduct."

This exquisite preparation pays wonderfully at the climactic moment of the novel, when Elizabeth reconsiders the letter in which Darcy justified his conduct toward Bingley and Jane and Wickham. Since more kindly views of Darcy have been introduced through the flow of witty talk, Darcy does not at that point have to be remade, but merely reread. (The tendency to remake a character appears in an obvious form only in the later and lesser scenes of the novel.)

The passages in which Elizabeth reviews the letter present an odd, rather legalistic process. After the more obvious views of Darcy's behavior and the possible alternatives are directly stated, the evidence on both sides is weighed and a reasonable conclusion is reached:

> After wandering along the lane for two hours, giving way to every variety of thought; re-considering events, determining probabilities, and reconciling herself as well as she could, to a change so sudden and so important, fatigue, and a recollection of her long absence, made her at length return home. . . .

To illustrate her manner of "determining probabilities" we might take one of several examples of Darcy's pride. Immediately after Darcy has proposed to her, she describes his treatment of Jane in rather brutal language:

> . . . his pride, his abominable pride, his shameless avowal of what he had done with respect to Jane, his unpardonable assurance in acknowledging, though he could not justify it.

A little later, she rereads the passage in which Darcy explains that Jane had shown no "symptom of peculiar regard" for Bingley. A second perusal reminds Elizabeth that Charlotte Lucas had a similar opinion, and she acknowledges the justice of this account of Jane's outward behavior. In much the same way she reviews other charges, such as Darcy's unfairness to Wickham or his objection to her family's "want of importance," and she is forced by the new evidence to draw "more probable" conclusions.

Jane Austen does not make us suppose that Elizabeth has now discovered the real Darcy or that an intricate person is easily known or known in his entirety, as is very clearly shown by Elizabeth's reply to Wickham's ironic questions about Darcy:

> "I dare not hope," he continued in a lower and more serious tone, "that he is improved in essentials."
>
> "Oh, no!" said Elizabeth. "In essentials, I believe, he is very much what he ever was."
>
> While she spoke, Wickham looked as if scarcely knowing whether to rejoice over her words, or to distrust their meaning. There was a something in her countenance which made him listen with an apprehensive and anxious attention, while she added,
>
> "When I said that he improved on acquaintance, I did not mean that either his mind or manners were in a state of improvement, but that from knowing him better, his disposition was better understood."

It is wise not to be dogmatic about "essentials," since in any case they remain "as they were." A sensible person contents himself with "better understanding."

This process of judgment is not merely odd or legalistic, because it is dramatically appropriate. It fits exactly the double presentation of Darcy's character through ironic dialogue and comment, and it fits perfectly the picture of Elizabeth as "a rational creature speaking the truth from her heart," one who adapts her statements to her knowledge. She is quite clear about the meaning of "pride" and "vanity," and she judges herself with complete honesty:

> "Had I been in love, I could not have been more wretchedly blind. But vanity, not love, has been my folly.—Pleased with the preference of one, and offended by the neglect of the other, on the very beginning of our acquaintance, I have courted prepossession and ignorance, and driven reason away, where either were concerned. Till this moment, I never knew myself."

We feel that Elizabeth's judgment of Darcy and of herself is right because the preparation for it has been so complete. The foundations for Elizabeth's choices and her acknowledgment of error were laid in the ambiguous remarks of the earlier scenes of the novel.

The dialogue has been preparing us equally well and with perhaps greater refinement for Elizabeth's realization that she and Darcy now regard one another with very different feelings. The ironic remarks and commentary have included hints that revealed ever so gradually Darcy's developing interest in Elizabeth. Mr. Darcy's "politeness," his "repeated questions," his "gallantry," his "look of doubt," if interpreted favorably, indicate his increasing warmth of feeling. Elizabeth's pert remarks and impertinent questions bear an amusing relation to this change in Darcy's sentiments. Besides being more ambiguous than she supposes, they backfire in another way, by increasing Darcy's admiration. Her accusation of "premeditated contempt" brings out his most gallant reply, and her "mixture of sweetness and archness" leaves him more "bewitched" than ever. In this and other ways the repartee provides local "amusements" while pointing forward to the complete reversal of feeling that follows the meeting at Pemberley.

The judicial process by which Elizabeth earlier "determined probabilities" in judging Darcy's past conduct is matched by the orderly way in which she now "determines her feelings" toward him:

> . . . and the evening, though as it passed it seemed long, was not long enough to determine her feelings towards *one* in that mansion; and she lay awake two whole hours, endeavouring to make them out. She certainly did not hate him. No; hatred had vanished long ago, and she had almost as long been ashamed of ever feeling a dislike against him, that could be so called. The respect created by the conviction of his valuable qualities, though at first unwillingly admitted, had for some time ceased to be repugnant to her feelings; and it was now heightened into somewhat of a

friendlier nature, by the testimony so highly in his favour, and bringing forward his disposition in so amiable a light, which yesterday had produced. But above all, above respect and esteem, there was a motive within her of good will which could not be overlooked. It was gratitude.—Gratitude, not merely for having once loved her, but for loving her still well enough, to forgive all the petulance and acrimony of her manner in rejecting him, and all the unjust accusations accompanying her rejection. He who, she had been persuaded, would avoid her as his greatest enemy, seemed, on this accidental meeting, most eager to preserve the acquaintance, and without any indelicate display of regard, or any peculiarity of manner, where their two selves only were concerned, was soliciting the good opinion of her friends, and bent on making her known to his sister. Such a change in a man of so much pride, excited not only astonishment but gratitude—for to love, ardent love, it must be attributed; and as such its impression on her was of a sort to be encouraged, as by no means unpleasing, though it could not be exactly defined. She respected, she esteemed, she was grateful to him, she felt a real interest in his welfare. . . .

In this beautifully graded progress of feeling, from "hatred" or any "dislike" to "respect" to "esteem" to "gratitude" and "a real interest" in Darcy's "welfare," each sentiment is defined with an exactness that is perfectly appropriate to Elizabeth's habit of mind as presented earlier in the novel. She defines her sentiments as exactly as her moral judgments.

As all ambiguities are resolved and all irony is dropped, the reader feels the closing in of a structure by its necessary end, the end implied in the crude judgment of Darcy in the first ballroom scene. The harsh exhibit of the way character is decided in this society prepares us to view Mr. Darcy's later actions as open to more than one interpretation:

. . . Mr. Darcy soon drew the attention of the room by his fine, tall person, handsome features, noble mien; and the report which was in general circulation within five minutes after his entrance, of his having ten thousand a year. The gentlemen pronounced him to be a fine figure of a man, the ladies declared he was much handsomer than Mr. Bingley, and he was looked at with great admiration for about half the evening, till his manners gave a disgust which turned the tide of his popularity; for he was discovered to be proud, to be above his company, and above being pleased; and not all his large estate in Derbyshire could then save him from having a most forbidding, disagreeable countenance, and being unworthy to be compared with his friend.

. . . His character was decided. He was the proudest, most disagreeable man in the world, and everybody hoped that he would never come there again.

These comments convey above all the aloof vision of the ironist, of Jane Austen herself, who had been described years before as a little girl "who is a judge of character and who remains silent." In the very grammar of the sentences (the passive voice, the *oratio obliqua*), there is an implication of a detached and superior mind that reports both judgments of Darcy, knowing quite well which is the more true, and fully aware that true judgment is considerably more difficult than most people suppose. The display of alternatives in ironic dialogue, the projection by this means of intricate characters, and the movement toward a sounder evaluation of first impressions—all this and more is implicit in the initial view of Darcy and his judges.

Once we have reached the scenes in which the promise of the introduction is fulfilled, the literary design both ironic and dramatic is complete. Thereafter, it must be admitted, *Pride and Prejudice* is not quite the same sort of book. There are fewer passages of equally bright and varied irony and consequently rarer exhibitions of intricacy of character. Mr. Darcy now appears as "humble," not "proud," and even as "perfectly amiable." There are single scenes of a broadly satiric sort, in which Mr. and Mrs. Bennet express characteristic opinions on their daughters' alliances and misalliances. But the close and harmonious relation between ironic wit and dramatic movement is disturbed. A great deal happens, from seductions and mysterious financial transactions to reunions of lovers and weddings. But these events seem to belong to a simpler world where outright judgments of good and bad or of happy and unhappy are in place. The double vision of the ironist is more rarely in evidence.

Occasionally, we feel a recovery of the richer texture of amusement and of the more complex awareness of character revealed in the central sequence. One glancing remark suggests that the final picture of Darcy might have been less simply ideal (Darcy has just been commenting on how well Bingley had taken his confession of having separated Bingley and Jane):

> Elizabeth longed to observe that Mr. Bingley had been a most delightful friend; so easily guided that his worth was invaluable; but she checked herself. She remembered that he had yet to learn to be laught at, and it was rather too early to begin. In anticipating the happiness of Bingley, which of course was to be inferior only to his own, he continued the conversation till they reached the house.

It is perhaps not "rational," as Elizabeth would say, to expect the same complexity when a drama of irony has once arrived at its resolution. But it is probably wise for the novelist to finish up his story as soon as possible after that point has been reached. In *Emma*, the crucial scene of readjustment comes very near the end of the novel. Jane Austen does not run the risk of presenting many scenes in which

Emma appears as a wiser and less fanciful young woman. To be sure, the risk is lessened somewhat because the initial and governing vision in Emma is less purely ironic than in *Pride and Prejudice.*

The triumph of *Pride and Prejudice* is a rare one, just because it is so difficult to balance a purely ironic vision with credible presentation of a man and woman undergoing a serious "change of sentiment." Shakespeare achieves an uneasy success in *Much Ado About Nothing,* and Fielding succeeds in *Tom Jones* because he does not expect us to take "love" too seriously. The problem for the writer who essays this difficult blend is one of creating dramatic speech which fulfils his complex intention. In solving this problem of expression, Jane Austen has her special triumph.

Jane Austen's *Pride and Prejudice* in the Eighteenth-Century Mode

by Samuel Kliger

I

It is no difficult task to cull from Jane Austen's *Pride and Prejudice* passages reflecting the period's taste in art and employing a critical terminology made widely current throughout the eighteenth century by many formal discussions of aesthetics. Thus, for example, two performances at the piano by Elizabeth Bennet, the heroine, and her sister Mary, are evaluated in terms of the familiar antithesis, drawn in innumerable essays of the period, between "art" and "nature." Elizabeth performs first and the author comments: "Her performance was pleasing, though by no means capital. After a song or two, and before she could reply to the entreaties of several that she would sing again, she was eagerly succeeded at the instrument by her sister Mary, who having, in consequence of being the only plain one in the family, worked hard for knowledge and accomplishments, was always impatient for display." As for the sister, however: "Mary had neither genius nor taste; and though vanity had given her application, it had given her likewise a pedantic air and conceited manner, which would have injured a higher degree of excellence than she had reached. Elizabeth, easy and unaffected, had been listened to with much more pleasure, though not playing half so well." [I, vi]

A century-long discussion, particularly of Shakespeare, is neatly summarized in this passage. Shakespeare, the period agreed, "wanted art"; but, his natural genius offsetting his neglect of art, he was exon-

"Jane Austen's Pride and Prejudice *in the Eighteenth-Century Mode"* *by Samuel Kliger. From* University of Toronto Quarterly, *XVI (1947), 357–71. Copyright © 1947 by the University of Toronto Press. Reprinted by permission of the University of Toronto Press and the author. The essay is somewhat shortened in the present edition, and references to the text of* Pride and Prejudice *have been standardized and moved to the body of the essay.*

erated. Mrs. Griffith, for example, condemned those "mechanists in criticism" who judged Shakespeare "by the cold rules of artful construction." She remarked further: "Would they restrain him within the precincts of art, the height, the depth of whose imagination and creative genius found even the extent of Nature too streightly bounded for it to move in?" [1] Pope, earlier in the century, had also declared for the "grace beyond the reach of art": "A cooler Judgment may commit fewer Faults, and be more approv'd in the Eyes of *One Sort* of Criticks: but that Warmth of Fancy will carry the loudest and more universal Applauses which holds the Heart of a Reader under the strongest Enchantment." [2]

These were critical commonplaces of the period. The contemporary reader of Jane Austen's novel would recognize at once the critical distinctions between "art" and "nature" involved and would concur, perhaps, in extending the palm not to Mary's artful yet unpleasing rendition but to Elizabeth's "natural" singing despite its obvious failures in the "art" of voice cultivation. On the other hand, however, although Jane Austen's partiality for Elizabeth's vivid style is obvious, it would be a serious mistake to conclude that it was possible for either Jane Austen or her period to deprecate "art" altogether. Nothing could be further from the truth of eighteenth-century aesthetic standards, generally speaking. The whole point of the art-nature antithesis was that it was usable as a basis for erecting an apparatus for the critical analysis of painting, literature, and the fine arts, which by manipulation of the two contraries, "art" and "nature," found excellence in a just mixture of these two opposing qualities. In this kind of analysis, faults were identified with excesses in any one extreme or exclusive emphasis on one extreme of style. The rationalistic temper of the period required that excellence be found in a mean between two extremes.[3] Only those readers persuaded by the false classic-romantic dichotomy embalmed in the simpler sort of literary text-books will find in Jane Austen's relative partiality for Elizabeth an absolute condemnation of Mary's "art." As

---

[1] Mrs. Elizabeth Griffith, *The Morality of Shakespeare's Drama Illustrated* (London, 1775), 26; cf. R. W. Babcock, *The Genesis of Shakespeare Idolatry* (Chapel Hill, N.C., 1931), 124-5.

[2] Pope, Preface to the translation of the *Iliad*; in W. H. Durham, *Critical Essays of the Eighteenth Century* (New Haven, 1915), 341.

[3] Cf. the brilliant article, from which I have quoted practically verbatim, by R. S. Crane, "English Criticism: Neo-classicism," in *Dictionary of World Literature*, ed. by Joseph T. Shipley (New York, 1943); Crane also quotes appositely from an eighteenth-century source: "The same just moderation must be observed in regard to ornaments; nothing will contribute more to destroy repose than profusion. . . . On the other hand, a work without ornament, instead of simplicity, to which it makes pretensions, has rather the appearance of poverty." (P. 198.)

a matter of fact, those who read the novel in this rigid manner will fail to see that by a kind of calculated ambiguity, Jane Austen has purposely set up in the singing scene two alternative possibilities of interpretation: i.e., Elizabeth's "naturalness" is either praiseworthy or to be condemned. Before the novel's end, it will become apparent that, one alternative removed, the remaining alternative fixes the conception of Elizabeth's character and attitudes.[4]

The contrast between Elizabeth's "natural" and Mary's "artful" rendition is soon extended, as anyone can expect who is even moderately well read in eighteenth-century aesthetic discussion, to involve a second set of terms, held in essential opposition: "reason" and "feeling." Thus Mary comments on Elizabeth's decision to walk the three miles to the Bingley home in order to investigate Jane's illness: "I admire the activity of your benevolence, . . . but every impulse of feeling should be guided by reason; and, in my opinion, exertion should always be in proportion to what is required." [I, vii] Art and reason are the terms on one side of the antithesis; nature and benevolence are the terms on the other side. The contextual shift along the line from "art" (a literary norm) to "reason" (an ethical norm) is readily recognizable as a commonplace in the neo-classical idea-complex. From Shaftesbury onwards, taste in art had almost invariably been conceived as a species of virtue. No notion was more characteristic of English neo-classicism than the idea that taste in the fine arts is an ally of morals. The eighteenth century believed that both the feeling for beauty and the prizing of what is decent and proper, perfect the character of the gentleman. As Alexander Gerard expressed it in his *Essay on Taste*: "A man of nice taste will have a stronger abhorrence of vice and a keener relish for virtue, in any given situation, than a person of dull organs can have in the same circumstances." [5] Because of the contextual shift or correlation of art with morals, Elizabeth's emotionalism is to be seen as the correlative of her artless singing. Furthermore, her indecorous behaviour, although clearly motivated by a warm devotion to her sick sister, Jane, also suggests, nevertheless, possibilities of censure, in that the century saw moral excellence as action conforming, as does good art, to a universal criterion of the mean between two extremes. In other words, Elizabeth's emotionalism is not only correlative to her natural style of singing but by calculated ambiguity is purposely presented in the novel in such a way as to suggest possibilities of both praise and

---

[4] Cf. Reuben A. Brower, "The Controlling Hand: Jane Austen and *Pride and Prejudice*" (*Scrutiny*, XIII, 1945, 99–111); Brower calls attention to this device of calculated ambiguity although he does not deal with the music episode.

[5] Quoted by W. G. Howard, "Good Taste and Conscience" (*PMLA*, XXV, 1910, 486–97).

censure. By means of this artistic device, the novel's end is practically dictated: that is, the period's rationalistic quest of the mean between two extremes requires that the probabilities for the heroine's behaviour be set up between two alternatives, neither of which is acceptable alone; the rejection of one alternative makes spectacularly clear to the heroine (and the reader) that the solution lies not in the remaining alternative but in a just moderation between the two.

In a third passage, the bi-polar terms "art" and "nature" reveal yet another tension in the neo-classical idea-complex, between "original-ity" (inspiration, spontaneity, singularity, enthusiasm, excess, the un-tutored genius—these are all synonymous in current critical usage) and the opposite of originality, the "rules" (regularity, uniformity, propriety, *bon sens,* the appeal to precedent and the example of Greek and Roman antiquity, the disciplined artist—these are all synonyms in the eighteenth-century vocabulary of criticism). The tension is brought to light in Mary's comment on Collins' letter: "In point of composition, . . . , his letter does not seem defective. The idea of the olive branch perhaps is not wholly new, yet I think it is well ex-pressed." [6] Mary's measured praise of Collins' epistolary style is in accord with Pope's dictum,

> True wit is Nature to advantage dress'd
> What oft was thought, but ne'er so well express'd,

as only one expression out of many of the period's critical viewpoint towards "originality." Jane Austen's contemporary readers, simply because their values were the same as Jane Austen's, did not need to be reminded, as does the modern reader, either of the critical distinc-tion between the term "originality" and its antithetical correlative "uniformity," or that these concepts were transvaluations of the basic antithesis between "art" and "nature." In the pattern, Mary is the sym-bol of art, reason, uniformity while Elizabeth is the symbol of nature, benevolence, originality.

The subject of letter-writing, in a fourth passage, causes a shift a second time in the narrative from art and nature, conceived unilater-ally in their aesthetic application, to the question of a universal stan-dard of excellence common to art and morals alike. Darcy is composing a letter and Miss Bingley, whose game it is to detract from Elizabeth's charm, monopolizes the conversation. In this sequence, Miss Bingley is twitting Darcy on his slow, laborious writing. In verbal parry and thrust, the information is elicited that Bingley, by contrast, is a rapid writer: "My ideas flow so rapidly that I have not time to express them; by which means my letters sometimes convey no ideas at all to my cor-

[6] Chap. xiii, 68.

respondents." [I, x] Elizabeth, who is only too eager to humble Darcy's pride—if she can—takes the occasion to praise Bingley's modesty in confessing his epistolary faults. Darcy, however, is not prone to accept her judgment, and he even condemns such modesty as a kind of hypocrisy. As the banter grows, it becomes clear that Darcy reproves "precipitance" (it is his own word) in letter-writing and in social conduct. The tie of friendship between Bingley and himself notwithstanding, there is no point, Darcy is saying, in shrinking from condemning Bingley's epistolary deficiencies. Darcy is offended by Bingley's epistolary improprieties as if they were moral misdemeanors—this, of course, is possible only because the period correlated art with morals. In addition, Darcy is arguing that Elizabeth is compounding the original error in seeking exculpation in friendship. Darcy's overbearing manner may be reprehensible, and before the novel's end he too will approach the mean and allow for the ties of friendship; but because of the century's rationalistic "religion," there is in his reprimand of Elizabeth and Bingley more of a defence of the universe's rational aims and goals than there is a defence of a purely literary standard. Propriety for Darcy is universal and immutable, imbedded in the rational scheme of things, or is, rather, the means of achieving life's rational ends.

Two additional passages, concentrating on Elizabeth's predilection for the artless, also reveal a background of eighteenth-century aesthetic discussion. One concerns the merits in landscape gardening as between the French trimmed garden and the English wild, natural garden, and the second, Longinus' theory of the "sublime." Mrs. Gardiner's invitation to Elizabeth to visit the Lake-country arouses Elizabeth's anticipations of pleasure in the sublimity of rocks and mountains: "What are men to rocks and mountains? Oh, what hours of transport we shall spend!" [II, iv] In the second passage, Elizabeth's visit to Pemberley, Darcy's family seat, opens to her enraptured eyes the beauty of Pemberley's natural landscaping. It was "without any artificial appearance. Its banks were neither formal nor falsely adorned. Elizabeth was delighted. She had never seen a place for which nature had done more, or where natural beauty had been so little counteracted by an awkward taste." [7] [III, i] In neither of these passages is the doctrine of "nature" extended to morals, but to the period, as we have seen, "nature" was simultaneously an aesthetic and ethical norm. "Transport," in particular, is a key word in the period to a protracted discussion of Longinus' theory of the "sublime." The transport afforded by rocks and mountains illustrates the interest in *beau désordre,* created by a

[7] For discussion of the eighteenth-century vogue in gardening and the critical principles invoked, see B. S. Allen, *Tides in English Taste* (2 vols.; Cambridge, Mass., 1937).

shift within the neo-classical thought-complex away from a doctrine of uniform nature, regular and orderly, toward a doctrine which saw excellence in irregularity; the concomitant shift was from reason to emotion, from a rational deistic religion to a religion of "enthusiasm." In other words, both ethical and aesthetic criteria were involved in the discussion of "art" and "nature." [8]

These are the passages on art criticism which *Pride and Prejudice* yields to the attentive reader. However, as we have already seen, it is a quite dubious procedure which would attempt to establish a partiality on Jane Austen's part for any one of the critical ideas which the novel expresses. Critical ideas introduced within the context of a novel are not at all the same as critical ideas expressed in a formal treatise on the subject. At any rate, even if we waive the objection, the search for typical eighteenth-century critical ideas in *Pride and Prejudice* would nevertheless tend to miss the whole point, which can be expressed in the following way: in both great and small plots, the novel intends to invoke the same thoughts and attitudes about the antithesis of art and nature. The concentration, in fact, in the small plot on singing, letter-writing, the enjoyment of mountainous sublimity, the appreciation of gardening, carries out Jane Austen's carefully premeditated plan for increasing the availability of the art-nature antithesis for the love plot or basic situation of the novel. In other words, the art-nature antithesis is abstracted into a symbolism adequate to cover the adventures and misadventures which keep Elizabeth and Darcy apart in mutual repulsion at the beginning of the tale and bring them together at the end. Instead, therefore, of selecting passages by an eclectic method in the interest of a systematic exposition of Jane Austen's views on art, the passages ought to be chosen by a formal method, treating the book as an art form with its own laws of development, in the interest of establishing the mutual appropriateness of the art-nature antithesis to the probabilities for action set up in the characters, who are arranged along a scale from one extreme of behaviour suggested by the

[8] The basic studies of the entire question, in addition to Professor Crane's excellent condensation already referred to, are by Arthur O. Lovejoy: "The Parallel of Deism and Classicism" (*Modern Philology*, XXIX, 1932, 281–99); "Optimism and Romanticism" (*PMLA*, XLII, 1927, 921–45); " 'Nature' as an Aesthetic Norm" (*Modern Language Notes*, 1927, 444–50). For a discussion of the interest in the *beau désordre* of mountains see Claire Engel, *La Littérature alpestre en France et en Angleterre* (Chambéry, 1930); however for strictures on Mlle Engel's oversimplification of the multivocality of the term "nature," precisely the question raised by Jane Austen's *Pride and Prejudice*, see the book reviewed in *Philological Quarterly*, XI, 1930, 175–7. For a typical statement, correlating taste and the moral sense, see Shaftesbury, *Characteristics*, ed. by J. M. Robertson (London, 1900), I, 262.

terms art and reason to the extreme at the opposite end of the scale suggested by the terms nature and emotion.

The purpose of this essay, therefore, is first to establish the art-nature antithesis as the ground of the book's action and its mode of organization and, second, to show that the doctrine of art and reason is extended to morals, to include, in particular, a concept of class relationships. Darcy's pride of class is persistently misunderstood by Elizabeth and what she must learn is that his pride—under proper limitations—is appropriate and a proper human trait. Contrariwise, Darcy must learn that Elizabeth's prejudice for dealing with humans *qua* humans, irrespective of class, is—again under proper limitations—appropriate and an admirable human trait. Thus between the problem posed in the initial scenes of the novel and its resolution at the book's end is a dialectic which separates the two leading characters in the beginning and joins them at the end in a mean between the two extremes which each respectively represents. Jane Austen has a host of admirers, but it seems merely idle to praise her perfection of form without being able to indicate in specific ways how the perfection is achieved. The governing idea of *Pride and Prejudice* is the art-nature antithesis; the perfection of form is achieved through relating each character and incident to the basic art-nature dialectic. A concentration on the art-nature contrast at the book's beginning in the sequence describing Mary's art and Elizabeth's artlessness prepares the reader to recognize that it is precisely the same dialectic between whose ebb and flow Elizabeth and Darcy, in their conflicting attitudes towards class relationships, gyrate. Tracing the art-nature dialectic will give clearer meaning to *Pride and Prejudice* and will show how completely dedicated Jane Austen was to the art of fiction.

II

The ethical expression of the art-nature opposition which governs the novel appears in an antithesis between primitivism and society. The reader of Jane Austen's novel should recall that because of a vogue in the eighteenth century of primitivistic discussion, the term "nature" had also established itself as one item of an antithesis on another level between the "arts" (man-made) and that which is in "nature" (God-made); the antithesis could be used to indicate whether civilization was progressing from the primitive state of nature because of man's progress in the arts, manufactures, organized government, and private property; or, conversely, whether civilization was retrograding because the arts, manufactures, government, and private property represented a perversion of nature. Elizabeth's prejudice toward Darcy's pride of class, her insistence on dealing with humans *qua* humans (naturally, that is) express the ideas at the primitivistic pole of the antithesis; Darcy is the spokesman for civilization, man-made and not in "nature," especially as he speaks in terms of a theory of class stratification. Elizabeth represents "man-in-nature," the earlier felicity and joy existing in the class-less, government-less, property-less conditions surrounding men in the Garden of Eden before the Fall. Darcy represents the consequences of the fall of man, the arts of society and government necessary to restrain the wickedness and greed of men resulting from their fall from the bliss of Eden. In Darcy culminates a centuries-old tradition, carefully nurtured by Christian thinkers throughout the medieval period and carried down to modern times without significant change. . . .

III

We are now at the heart of the Elizabeth-Darcy problem. The issues are clear: (1) A tension is created between the conceptions of man-in-nature and man-in-society; the first deals with humans *qua* humans, the second deals with humans as the "art" of society directs their activities. (2) Pride in class is a proper and justifiable human trait; superiority, so far from being a usurped right, is actually a heavy burden of duties which one assumes; the essential meaning of *noblesse oblige* is this willingness to serve. (3) Since no class exists for itself but is bound by reciprocated rights and duties to classes above and below, social non-compliance is represented either in improper respect for classes above or in delinquency in duty to classes below. (4) The system embodies the universal criterion of the mean between the two extremes; the individual's worth *qua* individual is adjusted to his worth as a member of a social class, whatever his class may be; a dialectic separates the natural man from man as the art of society has created him; nature and art are the juxtaposed terms. Considering the dialectic which separates the two terms, it is instructive to observe how the great Renaissance rationalist, Bishop Hooker, formulated the problem. He pointed out that individuals who are perfectly exemplary are not necessarily the same considered as members of society: "It is both commonly said, and truly, that the best men otherwise are not always the best in regard of society. The reason whereof is, for that the law of men's actions is one, if they be respected only as men; and another, when they are considered as parts of a public body. Many men there are, than whom nothing is more commendable when they

are singled; and yet in society with others none less fit to answer the
duties which are looked for at their hands." [9]

Since it is Darcy who capitulates first and early in the book, the real
concern of the author is evidently Elizabeth's quest of the mean between the two extremes of "art" and "nature." It is Elizabeth who must
set her emotional house in order and learn to evaluate all that has
happened to her in terms of the mean between the two extremes of the
"art" of human relationships and humans in their "natural" associa-
tions. In Bishop Hooker's terms, she is an exemplary person as an
individual, but she is socially deficient. On the other hand, Darcy is
socially exemplary but is deficient in naturalness.

In the letter-writing scene, resentful of Darcy's stiff-necked pride,
Elizabeth scores a point for herself, although ostensibly she is defend-
ing Bingley's relaxed epistolary style against Darcy's condemnation of
such indecorum. She says: "You appear to me, Mr. Darcy, to allow
nothing for the influence of friendship and affection." [I, x] Elizabeth
may be right, but she may be wrong also. Darcy scores a point for
reason and the "art" of human relationships when he replies: "Pride
—where there is a real superiority of mind—pride will always be
under good regulation." [I, xi] Pride, he is saying, is a proper human
trait; but Elizabeth is scornful. Her prejudice for dealing with humans
qua humans, irrespective of class standards, naturally instead of artfully, emotionally instead of rationally, has nearly fatal consequences
for her in so far as it almost brings her to a marriage with Wickham.

Wickham precipitates the main action. In the first place, he raises
the crucial problem of reciprocated rights and duties. The question is
whether the Darcys, father and son, have been true to their class mission of rewarding a faithful servitor. Slyly but shrewdly, Wickham
encourages Elizabeth to believe that the younger Darcy has been
remiss in his social duties. The entire incident is revealing not only
of Wickham's rascality but of Darcy's class idealism and of Elizabeth's
failure to consider more sympathetically Darcy's class pride which
debars him from expostulating even when he has been seriously
libelled.

The fundamental principle of *noblesse oblige* is never to complain,
never to explain. No gentleman will either complain or explain when
his actions are falsely reported. It is beneath Darcy's pride to explain
that Wickham had signed away for cash his right to the Darcy patronage. Darcy by his attitude acknowledges the merit of the phrase *"honi
soit qui mal y pense"*—and it is certainly part of Elizabeth's later
humiliation that she must recognize her failure to understand Darcy's

---

[9] Bishop Hooker, *Of the Laws of Ecclesiastical Politie,* ed. by R. W. Church (Oxford, 1896), I. xvi. 6, pp. 103–4.

silence. With perfect consistency, Darcy afterwards serves Elizabeth silently and well in the Lydia-Wickham elopement by removing the financial obstacles in the way of the marriage. On the other hand, Wickham further displays his lack of principles in his loud complaints to Elizabeth.

Elizabeth falls victim to Wickham's strategy only because of her prejudice for dealing with people naturally, irrespective of class. It is characteristic of her that she seeks to measure Darcy for human consistency and she fails for the obvious reason that she is measuring him with the wrong measuring stick. This is brought out in her reply to Wickham that, granting Darcy his pride, his pride alone should have encouraged him to discharge his class obligation to his former steward: "How strange! . . . How abominable! I wonder that the very pride of this Mr. Darcy has not made him just to you! If from no better motive, that he should not have been too proud to be dishonest—for dishonesty I must call it." [I, xvi]

In a chastened spirit, Elizabeth learns to respect Darcy's pride of class. Her surrender is expressed explicitly in the words which she intends to remove her father's anxiety about her impending marriage with Darcy: "I love him. Indeed he has no improper pride." [III, xvii] A complete surrender of either Darcy or Elizabeth to the other would completely falsify the eighteenth century's ideal of moderation and would obscure the basic art-nature antithesis. As it is, the partial capitulation of each to the other makes clear that each recognizes that every quality has its corresponding defect. With a sudden pleasant surprise, the reader recalls that early in the novel, Jane Austen, with an irony that must have been deliberate, suggests the idea as the premise upon which in the central sequence of the novel the quest proceeds for the mean between extremes when she has Darcy say: "There is, I believe, in every disposition a tendency to some particular evil, a natural defect, which not even the best education can overcome." [I, xi] The exposure of Wickham's perfidy makes Elizabeth, as she reflects backwards on her wilful misunderstanding of Darcy's class idealism, realize her defect of considering people exclusively in their natural relations with corresponding neglect of their opposite qualities arising out of their social relations as the arts of government and society shape them.

It is not intended to suggest that Elizabeth is a doctrinaire revolutionary, aiming to level all classes. There is not a single statement in the novel which can be construed as politically tendentious. On this score alone, the critics are quite right who point out that Jane Austen was totally unaffected by the currents of thought set up by the French Revolution; not even her relative residing in her house, whose husband was beheaded by the guillotine, moved her to interpret the Revolution. Yet *Pride and Prejudice* is not merely a mild satire on manners but, as we have seen, hands down a social verdict. The satire in the novel on social institutions hardly ripples the surface, but the currents underneath are powerful. If the conclusion of the novel makes clear that Elizabeth accepts class relationships as valid, it becomes equally clear that Darcy, through Elizabeth's genius for treating all people with respect for their natural dignity, is reminded that institutions are not an end in themselves but are intended to serve the end of human happiness. . . .

IV

It is perhaps already apparent how the art-nature antithesis is basic to the novel, every character and incident standing in expressive relationship to the concept.

Wickham as we have seen brings the problem of the "art" of class to a sharp focal point. But even more important to the basic scheme of the novel, joining all its parts in a coherent whole, is the interesting parallel between Wickham and Mrs. Bennet. Mr. Bennet is intellectually superior to his fatuous wife and unhappily wedded. If we question why he married his wife in the first place, we find an exact parallel to the Elizabeth-Wickham romance. Mr. Bennet must have responded to his wife's "natural" charms as a young girl. But since education or breeding, or what we may call "art," has added nothing to her natural charm, Mrs. Bennet lacks the just mixture of the opposing qualities of "art" and "nature." In exactly the same way, Elizabeth is attracted by Wickham's natural gaiety and charm. His nature, however, is impervious to breeding and gentlemanly virtue. Obviously the point is that had Elizabeth married Wickham, her fate would have been a copy of her father's. Her married life would have been as desolate as her father's of companionship worthy of respect.

The two hoydens, Lydia and Kitty, are fitted into the basic scheme in a very obvious way. They are feather-brained and totally irresponsible. No amount of breeding or "art" would ever correct their natures. Only Mr. Bennet's grim watchfulness to prevent a second catastrophe will probably save Kitty from her own natural waywardness.

Lady Catherine de Bourgh presents another variant of the class concept. She is born to her class, as is Darcy, but she represents merely the husk of the doctrine of class, not its inner living spirit. Her arrogant demands that Elizabeth give up Darcy reveal that her mind has been brutalized rather than stimulated to kindness by her notion of her class mission. The "art" of human relationships of which she is a devotee has no really human bearings whatsoever. She enters into the plan of the novel in a second way by creating a parallel with Darcy. The fact of the case clearly is that Lady Catherine represents what Darcy might have become, his pride of class hardening into brutality, had not Darcy met Elizabeth and had he not learned from her to soften his astringent class idealism with human kindness for people in their natural dignity.

Collins' fatuous adoration of aristocracy is acidly etched in such a way as to expose the fault of exclusive emphasis on class with neglect of the opposite quality of "nature." He is a class-casuist who empties the ideal of any meaning.

Jane and Bingley are also related to the novel's sequence of ideas as they are determined by the art-nature antithesis. Jane and Bingley have natural compatibilities for one another. Essentially benevolent, the problem of "art" superadding to their "natural" qualities is obviated altogether.

Dull, moralizing Mary is doomed to spinsterhood. She is usually omitted from most critical commentaries on the novel. In fact, Barker, in his *History of the English Novel*, calls her a "missfire," unrelated to the plot.[10] Actually, however, she is made to carry out the important office of introducing strategically into the novel, by way of a contrast with Elizabeth, the pole of "art" in the art-nature antithesis. The shallow currents which Mary sets in motion draw Elizabeth to powerful eddies at the centre of the novel.

Jane Austen's consciousness of tradition and moral values is as acute as her sense of the perilous disunity of life is deep. But to the extent to which novelists of other periods have also taken as their theme the disunity created by the clash of reason and emotion, conventions and instinct, officialdom and individualism, civilization and nature, it can be argued with reason that it is not essential to the understanding of *Pride and Prejudice* to recognize its eighteenth-century mode. Owen Wister's *The Virginian* may be taken as an example. The clash between the prim morality of the New England school-marm, Molly Wood, and the instinct or pragmatism of the cowboy who gives the novel its title, represents, more or less, the same conflict which disturbs Elizabeth and Darcy. The objection may be allowed to stand, yet we cannot dispense with the historical approach for the important reason that it is the historical approach which lays bare the novel as an art-form. A comparison of *Pride and Prejudice* with Mrs. Inchbald's *Nature and Art* (1795) will make the point clear.

[10] Vol. VI (London, 1935), 89.

The eighteenth century's specific formulation of the art-nature antithesis is basic to both novels. Yet when one decants from the surface of Mrs. Inchbald's novel the art-nature ideas, one discovers—without surprise—that nothing is left, her novel is merely a tract, and there is, consequently, hardly any question of its art. The same operation on *Pride and Prejudice,* on the other hand, also takes everything away but, paradoxically, leaves everything behind. The historical reconstruction can indeed be separated from, and, in fact, should precede, literary criticism; otherwise, the critic may be ignorant of relevant information, unaware of changed conventions, and caught up in modern democratic prejudices. The important things are to prevent irrelevant criticism of the eighteenth century's seriously pondered theory of social stratification, and to note the novel's context of moral values not as students of moral philosophy (this could be studied as well or even better in Mrs. Inchbald's tract) but as art critics; i.e., to note the appropriateness of the eighteenth century's favorite art-reason dialectic to a specific satirical method which finds its fictional types now dialectically separated at extremes and now dialectically brought together in a mean of behaviour between extremes. The satirical method, that is, is predetermined by prevailing eighteenth-century intellectual assumptions, preconceptions, and moral sanctions in a way unavailable to Owen Wister's *The Virginian* except as the latter faintly echoes ideas first discussed with greater seriousness during the "enlightenment" of the eighteenth century.

Into the Nineteenth Century: *Pride and Prejudice*

by A. Walton Litz

With *Pride and Prejudice* Jane Austen bid farewell to her early life and to the eighteenth century. We have seen that the recasting of *Sense and Sensibility* in 1809–11 never reached the vital centers of that novel; the original antitheses and conventions protrude through the final structure. But the late revisions of *Pride and Prejudice* (c. 1811–12) were so elaborate, and penetrated so deeply into the novel's language and action, that they amounted to a re-seeing of the entire work. Although it is impossible to reconstruct the details of *First Impressions*, we can say with some assurance that the finished novel was far removed from this early draft. Ten days after the publication of *Pride and Prejudice* Jane Austen wrote to Cassandra: "I am exceedingly pleased that you can say what you do, after having gone thro' the whole work." [1] This remark, as Mary Lascelles has pointed out, suggests a substantial difference between *First Impressions* and the published novel, since Jane Austen would have long been familiar with Cassandra's opinions of the early version. [2] Another indication of the extent of the revisions may be found in the elaborate use of the 1811–12 almanacs; the consistency of the novel's time-scheme could only have resulted from a thorough reworking of the plot. [3] But more important than this historical evidence is the general evidence of the novel's style, which is more uniform and sophisticated than that of *Sense and Sensibility*. In recasting *Sense and Sensibility* Jane Austen was doing the best job she could with a work already moribund in

---

"*Into the Nineteenth Century:* Pride and Prejudice." *From* Jane Austen: A Study of Her Artistic Development *by A. Walton Litz (New York: Oxford University Press, 1965), pp. 97–111. Copyright © 1965 by A. Walton Litz. Reprinted by permission of Oxford University Press, Inc.*

[1] *Letters [Jane Austen's Letters to Her Sister Cassandra and Others*, Second Edition, ed. R. W. Chapman (London: Oxford University Press, 1952)], 9 February 1813.

[2] [Mary] Lascelles [*Jane Austen and Her Art* (Oxford: Clarendon Press, 1939)], p. 31.

[3] See the Appendix on the Chronology of *Pride and Prejudice* in *Works* [Third Edition, ed. R. W. Chapman (London: Oxford University Press, 1932)], Vol. II.

her imagination. But *Pride and Prejudice* remained alive for her, its hero and heroine perpetually interesting.[4] On 24 May 1813, after a visit to "the Exhibition in Spring Gardens" held by the Society of Painters in Oil and Water Colours, she wrote to Cassandra:

> It is not thought a good collection, but I was very well pleased—particularly (pray tell Fanny) with a small portrait of Mrs. Bingley, excessively like her. I went in hopes of seeing one of her Sister, but there was no Mrs. Darcy;—perhaps however, I may find her in the Great Exhibition which we shall go to, if we have time . . . Mrs. Bingley's is exactly herself, size, shaped face, features & sweetness; there never was a greater likeness. She is dressed in a white gown, with green ornaments, which convinces me of what I had always supposed, that green was a favourite colour with her. I dare say Mrs. D. will be in Yellow.

And later in the same letter:

> We have been both to the Exhibition & Sir J. Reynolds',—and I am disappointed, for there was nothing like Mrs. D. at either. I can only imagine that Mr. D. prizes any Picture of her too much to like it should be exposed to the public eye.—I can imagine he w^d have that sort of feeling —that mixture of Love, Pride & Delicacy.[5]

It would seem that *Pride and Prejudice* remained fresh and exciting in Jane Austen's imagination for two reasons: first, the charm of the heroine, "as delightful a creature as ever appeared in print";[6] and second, her pleasure in having successfully reformed the original story to accord with her new ideals in theme and technique. We cannot think of *Pride and Prejudice* as belonging to any one period of Jane Austen's life before 1813; rather it was a summing up of her artistic career, a valedictory to the world of *Sense and Sensibility* and a token of things to come. More than any other of her novels it deserves Henry Austen's description in his Biographical Notice: "Some of these novels had been the gradual performances of her previous life." [7] One index to the new tones and new attitudes struck in *Pride and Prejudice* is the novel's use of conventions and stock situations drawn from eighteenth-century fiction. Both *Sense and Sensibility* and *Pride and Prejudice* depend upon characters and actions inherited from the

---

[4] Mary Lascelles remarks [p. 30] that *Sense and Sensibility* "was never to account for as much, to the author or her family, as the later novels: she would—'if asked'—tell them what became of Miss Steele, but her own imagination did not linger in the world of *Sense and Sensibility* as it was to do in that of *Pride and Prejudice*."

[5] *Letters,* 24 May 1813.

[6] *Letters,* 29 January 1813.

[7] *Works,* Vol. V. p. 4.

Richardson-Fanny Burney tradition: the attractive seducer, the thoughtless young hoyden, ill-mannered relatives, tyrannical aristocrats, elopements and assignations. It is obvious from the *Juvenilia* that Jane Austen recognized the potential absurdity of these conventions; but they were so much a part of her fictional experience, and in some cases so close to the actual world she knew, that she could not exclude them from her art. The superiority of *Pride and Prejudice* to *Sense and Sensibility* lies in the transformation of these stale conventions, which renders them a believable part of the action and a natural vehicle for the novel's themes. This difference may be seen in a comparison of the heroes and villains, Darcy with Colonel Brandon, Wickham with Willoughby. In *Sense and Sensibility* Colonel Brandon has no more life than Lord Orville in Funny Burney's *Evelina;* we believe in what he represents, but not in him. Yet Darcy, while preserving the virtues of the fictional hero, is entirely believable, since Jane Austen has subjected him to a process of self-evaluation and self-recognition. In him the type has been revivified. Similarly, the story of Willoughby's past behavior (as told by Colonel Brandon) is merely a plot device, a tale of seduction borrowed from fiction in the hope that it will give Willoughby's villainy substance and shape. In fact the tale stamps Willoughby as a two-dimensional figure; it substitutes his prototype in *Evelina* for the man we have glimpsed earlier, and not even the moving final confession can reassert his reality. But in *Pride and Prejudice* Wickham, although a descendant of the eighteenth-century fictional rake, does not suffer from the defects of his originals: his elopement with Lydia is plausible and carefully prepared, not a stale convention dragged in to forward the plot; and Darcy's account of Wickham's past villainies, unlike Colonel Brandon's tale, seems consonant with all we know of the subject's character.

It is important to keep these distinctions between *Sense and Sensibility* and *Pride and Prejudice* in mind when we speak of the latter's origins in late eighteenth-century fiction. Jane Austen's admiration of Fanny Burney is well known, and there can be no doubt that *Pride and Prejudice*—or, more exactly, *First Impressions*—owed a debt to *Cecilia*.[8] Q. D. Leavis exaggerates this debt in her statement that "the original conception of *First Impressions* was undoubtedly to rewrite

[8] For discussion of the relationship between Fanny Burney and Jane Austen, and between *Cecilia* and *Pride and Prejudice*, see C. L. Thomson, *Jane Austen*, London, 1929, pp. 100–106; Elizabeth Jenkins, *Jane Austen*, New York, 1949, pp. 49–57; Q. D. Leavis, "A Critical Theory of Jane Austen's Writings," *Scrutiny*, X (June 1941), 71–2; and R. W. Chapman's Appendix to *Works*, Vol. II. *Evelina* (1778) and *Cecilia* (1782) were well known to Jane Austen before she began *First Impressions* (1796), and *Camilla* was published in that year (with Jane Austen as one of the subscribers).

the story of Cecilia in realistic terms," [9] but we know that when Jane
Austen began work on the story the world of *Evelina* and *Cecilia*
held a great reality for her. A niece recollected hearing, as a very
young child, Jane Austen "read a part out of *Evelina,* one of the
chapters concerning the Branghtons and Mr. Smith, and she thought
it sounded like a play." [10] Fanny Burney's fiction is filled with figures
who remind us of Colonel Brandon or Willoughby or Lydia or Mrs.
Bennet, and although one can argue that these were common types,
the details of their treatment in Jane Austen's early work are often
reminiscent of Fanny Burney. More significantly, the struggle between
personal affection and family pride in *Cecilia* may have suggested the
major themes of *Pride and Prejudice;* certainly the title was taken
from the conclusion to *Cecilia,* where Dr. Lyster points the story's
moral.

"The whole of this unfortunate business . . . has been the result of
PRIDE and PREJUDICE. . . . Yet this, however, remember; if to PRIDE and
PREJUDICE you owe your miseries, so wonderfully is good and evil bal-
anced, that to PRIDE and PREJUDICE you will also owe their termination."

But these similarities between *Pride and Prejudice* and Fanny Burney's novels only intensify our sense of Jane Austen's achievement in
transforming the conventions of "the land of fiction." Since the limited
social world she observed had been the subject of so much previous
fiction, she was prevented from seeking originality in new situations
and new locales. Instead she had to find her voice within the same
range of life explored by many other female writers. Bingley's arrival
at Netherfield, the ballroom scene, Wickham's flirtations, Darcy's letter, Lydia's elopement, Lady Catherine's condescending visit—these
were standard raw materials, but in *Pride and Prejudice* they were
endowed with such a quantity of "felt life," and incorporated so skill-
fully into the drama, that they took on a new significance. It is this
transformation of familiar materials which yields one of the novel's
chief pleasures, the sense of subtle variations within a fixed and traditional range of experience. *Pride and Prejudice* bears that hallmark
of "classic" art, the discovery of new possibilities within a traditional
form.

Although the phrase "Pride and Prejudice" does not suggest as neat
an ideological antithesis as "Sense and Sensibility," it would have led
a late eighteenth-century reader to expect a schematic drama in which
each quality is represented by a separate character or faction. But in
Pride and Prejudice one cannot equate Darcy with Pride, or Elizabeth

⁹ Leavis, op. cit. p. 71.
¹⁰ Jenkins, op. cit. p. 51.

with Prejudice; Darcy's pride of place is founded on social prejudice, while Elizabeth's initial prejudice against him is rooted in pride of her own quick perceptions. In this we have a clear indication of the novel's distance from *Cecilia*, for Jane Austen's "internalizing" of the conflicts between proper and improper pride, candor and prejudice, goes far beyond the capabilities of Fanny Burney. Indeed, it was this ability to vest the novel's conflicts in the dynamic development of personality that freed Jane Austen from the world of static values which still dominates in *Sense and Sensibility*. Whereas in *Sense and Sensibility* the antitheses are resolved by a suppression of one position and an uneasy exaltation of the other, the entire movement of *Pride and Prejudice* tends toward a resolution of conflicts which is a union rather than a compromise, a union in which both parties gain new vigor and freedom of expression. The marriage of Elizabeth and Darcy resolves not only their personal differences but the conflicts they have represented, with the result that the novel provides a final pleasure unique in Jane Austen's fiction, a sense of complete fulfillment analogous to that which marks the end of some musical compositions. It is this sense of a union of opposites—without injury to the identity of either—which prompts the common comparison with Mozart. In *Pride and Prejudice*, for once in her career, Jane Austen allowed the symmetry of her imaginative creation to prevail over the protests of her social self, and the result is a triumph of ideal form. It was a triumph not to be repeated, one that was replaced in the later novels by less comforting views of human nature. Yet it remains valid as the finest expression of one aspect of Jane Austen's personality, her desire to endow human behavior with the order and symmetry of art. *Pride and Prejudice* is a great comedy because it formulates an ideal vision of human possibilities; its ending is "realistic" not because we measure the union of Elizabeth and Darcy against our own experience (that experience which delights in Jane Austen's statement that Mrs. Bennet remained "occasionally nervous and invariably silly"), but because their marriage is a complete fulfillment of the novel's artistic imperatives. Their lives have been the work's structure, and their marriage is a vindication of the artist's power to resolve complexities.

In his penetrating essay on *Mansfield Park* Lionel Trilling defines the special quality that distinguishes *Pride and Prejudice* from Jane Austen's other works.

> The great charm, the charming greatness, of *Pride and Prejudice* is that it permits us to conceive of morality as style. The relation of Elizabeth Bennet to Darcy is real, is intense, but it expresses itself as a conflict and reconciliation of styles: a formal rhetoric, traditional and rigorous,

must find a way to accommodate a female vivacity, which in turn must recognize the principled demands of the strict male syntax. The high moral import of the novel lies in the fact that the union of styles is accomplished without injury to either lover.[11]

Pride and Prejudice does more than testify to the artist's capacity for organizing and clarifying the confusions of life; it supports the fine illusion that life itself can take on the discrimination and selectivity of art. Throughout the novel aesthetic and moral values are closely related. Darcy and Elizabeth share the common eighteenth-century assumption that a man of real taste is usually a man of sound moral judgment,[12] and when Elizabeth first views Pemberley the tasteful prospect confirms her altered opinion of Darcy's character:

> Elizabeth's mind was too full for conversation, but she saw and admired every remarkable spot and point of view. They gradually ascended for half a mile, and then found themselves at the top of a considerable eminence, where the wood ceased, and the eye was instantly caught by Pemberley House, situated on the opposite side of a valley, into which the road with some abruptness wound. It was a large, handsome, stone building, standing well on rising ground, and backed by a ridge of high woody hills;—and in front, a stream of some natural importance was swelled into greater, but without any artificial appearance. Its banks were neither formal, nor falsely adorned. Elizabeth was delighted. She had never seen a place for which nature had done more, or where natural beauty had been so little counteracted by an awkward taste. They were all of them warm in their admiration; and at that moment she felt, that to be mistress of Pemberley might be something! (245) [III, i]

Every evidence of sound aesthetic judgment provided by Pemberley is converted by Elizabeth into evidence of Darcy's natural amiability, and joined with the enthusiastic testimony of the housekeeper, until Pemberley becomes an image of his true nature. Sir Walter Scott was not entirely imperceptive when he made his much-ridiculed remark that Elizabeth "does not perceive that she has done a foolish thing until she accidentally visits a very handsome seat and grounds belonging to her admirer." [13] Pemberley is more than a reminder of lost social and economic possibilities; it is a solid reflection of Elizabeth's new attitude toward Darcy.

[11] Lionel Trilling, *The Opposing Self*, New York, 1955, p. 222.

[12] Shaftesbury gave currency to the notion that the moral sense and the aesthetic sense spring from the same faculties. See William E. Alderman, "Shaftesbury and the Doctrine of Moral Sense in the Eighteenth Century," *PMLA*, XLVI (December 1931), 1087–94.

[13] Scott's review of *Emma* in the *Quarterly Review*, XIV (October 1815), 194.

This close connection between aesthetic and moral judgments enables Jane Austen to express her moral themes in terms of the novel's movement from complex antitheses to easy resolution. As Darcy and Elizabeth are first presented to us they sum up most of the conflicting forces in Jane Austen's early fiction. Elizabeth possesses the illusion of total freedom; she looks to nature, rather than society or traditional authority, for the basis of her judgments. She is self-reliant and proud of her discernment, contemptuous of all conventions that constrict the individual's freedom. Darcy, on the other hand, is mindful of his relationship to society, proud of his social place, and aware of the restrictions that inevitably limit the free spirit. Together they dramatize the persistent conflict between social restraint and the individual will, between tradition and self-expression.

Both Darcy and Elizabeth are flanked by figures who parody their basic tendencies: in Mr. Bennet the irony of the detached observer has become sterile, while Lady Catherine de Bourgh represents the worst side of aristocratic self-consciousness. But it is another group that provides the full antidote to pride and prejudice. The Gardiners stand as a rebuke to Darcy's social prejudices and aristocratic pride, an example of natural aristocracy; while Wickham's true nature is a telling blow to Elizabeth's pride of perception, and to her prejudice in favor of "natural" goodness. The marriage of Elizabeth and Darcy is, as Mark Schorer has pointed out, a kind of economic and social merging, an accommodation of traditional values based upon status with the new values personified in the Gardiners.[14] Elizabeth is led to an appreciation of Darcy's "proper" pride—"he has no improper pride," she ultimately protests to Mr. Bennet (376) [III, xvii]—while Darcy is disabused of his inherited prejudices based on caste and economic distance. But it would be too much to say, as Schorer does, that Jane Austen embodies her social judgments in Darcy, and her moral judgments in Elizabeth. For it is part of the novel's purpose to demonstrate that Elizabeth's original opinions were not freely arrived at, but conditioned by social prejudice, while Darcy's initial pride had its roots in a feeling of moral superiority. The first two volumes of *Pride and Prejudice* are so complex that no one set of antitheses can define the positions of the hero and heroine, and any attempt to establish rigid patterns leads to absurdity. Under such schematizing Darcy's ambivalent attitude is reduced to the promposity of Mary's extracts, while Elizabeth's wit becomes as sterile as her father's.

During recent years several intelligent critics have analyzed the stylistic and dramatic techniques used by Jane Austen to mark the

[14] Mark Schorer, "Pride Unprejudiced," *Kenyon Review*, XVIII (Winter 1956), 72–91.

subtle changes in the relationship between Darcy and Elizabeth.[15]
The most persuasive of these critics, Reuben Brower, has shown that
all of the surface wit and irony of the novel is *functional,* a part of
the larger dramatic design. Through a "sheer poetry of wit" Jane
Austen conveys multiple views of her major characters, yet never does
she lose sight of her fundamental dramatic aims. The greatness of the
novel—whatever its limitations may be—lies in her fusion of the
poetry of wit with the dramatic structure of fiction.[16] It is this combination of local complexity with a general clarity of design which
animates the novel, and redeems a story which could have been as
static as that of *Sense and Sensibility.* A perfect example of the organic
connection between language and action may be found in the speeches
of Elizabeth and Darcy, which change as the differences between them
are reconciled. In the novel's early scenes Jane Austen establishes a
clear-cut distinction between Elizabeth's lively speech and Darcy's
formal language, but this difference in expressive style is gradually
modified as each begins to appreciate the other's style of living. When
Darcy learns of the changes in Elizabeth's feelings toward him he expresses himself "as sensibly and as warmly as a man violently in love
can be supposed to do" (366) [III, xvi], while Elizabeth's defense of
her engagement to Mr. Bennet is reminiscent of Darcy's earlier remarks on the virtues of proper pride: "Indeed he has no improper
pride. He is perfectly amiable" (376) [III, xvii]. In the conventional
final chapter of *Pride and Prejudice,* where the future lives of the
characters are confidently charted, Jane Austen can summarize with
such easy authority because we have already seen these relationships
foreshadowed in the novel's language and action.

The foundation of Jane Austen's success in correlating language
and action is her irony, and the nature of this irony is nowhere better
displayed than in the permutations of the novel's first sentence: "It
is a truth universally acknowledged, that a single man in possession
of a good fortune, must be in want of a wife." Out of context this
general statement may seem no more significant than its original in
Rambler No. 115, where Hymenaeus writes:

"I was known to possess a fortune, and to want a wife; and therefore
was frequently attended by those hymeneal solicitors, with whose im-

[15] See Howard S. Babb, *Jane Austen's Novels: The Fabric of Dialogue,* Columbus,
1962, pp. 113–42; Reuben A. Brower, "Light and Bright and Sparkling: Irony and
Fiction in *Pride and Prejudice,*" in *The Fields of Light,* New York, 1951, pp. 164–81;
R. J. Schoeck, "Jane Austen and the Sense of Exposure: Heuristics in *Pride and
Prejudice,*" *English Studies,* XXXVI (August 1955), 154–7; and Dorothy Van
Ghent, *The English Novel: Form and Function,* New York, 1953, pp. 99–111.
[16] Brower, op. cit. especially pp. 164–5.

portunity I was sometimes diverted, and sometimes perplexed; for they contended for me as vultures for a carcase; each employing all his eloquence, and all his artifices, to enforce and promote his own scheme, from the success of which he was to receive no other advantage than the pleasure of defeating others equally eager, and equally industrious."

Yet even in isolation the novel's opening sentence contains a certain irony: the exaggeration of the statement jars against our sense of reality, and prepares us for the discovery in the first chapters of *Pride and Prejudice* that this "truth" is acknowledged only by Mrs. Bennet and her kind. In the context of these chapters the irony is directed at economic motives for marriage, but as the action develops the implications of the opening sentence are modified and extended, until by the end of the novel we are willing to acknowledge that both Bingley and Darcy were "in want of a wife." Thus the sentence is simultaneously a source for irony and a flat statement of the social and personal necessities which dominate the world of *Pride and Prejudice*. The basic truth of the generalization is untouched by its ironic potential, and this suggests an important distinction that must be made in any discussion of Jane Austen's mature art. Her irony is dramatic, not static; complex, not simple; and we can only judge the tenor of the author's comments or the professions of her characters against the total pattern of dramatic action. Take for an example the following dialogue between Darcy and Elizabeth:

"What think you of books?" said he, smiling.

"Books—Oh! no.—I am sure we never read the same, or not with the same feelings."

"I am sorry you think so; but if that be the case, there can at least be no want of subject.—We may compare our different opinions."

"No—I cannot talk of books in a ball-room; my head is always full of something else."

"The *present* always occupies you in such scenes—does it?" said he, with a look of doubt.

"Yes, always," she replied, without knowing what she said, for her thoughts had wandered far from the subject, as soon afterwards appeared by her suddenly exclaiming, "I remember hearing you once say, Mr. Darcy, that you hardly ever forgave, that your resentment once created was unappeasable. You are very cautious, I suppose, as to its *being created*."

"I am," said he, with a firm voice.

"And never allow yourself to be blinded by prejudice?"

"I hope not."

"It is particularly incumbent on those who never change their opinion, to be secure of judging properly at first."

"May I ask to what these questions tend?"

"Merely to the illustration of *your* character," said she, endeavouring to shake off her gravity. "I am trying to make it out." (93) [I, xviii]

By the time we have reached this passage in the novel we know enough of Darcy's nature, and Elizabeth's pride of judgment, to realize that the questions tend more to an illustration of *her* character than of his. In this exchange Jane Austen is depending on an immediate grasp of the inherent dramatic irony, and she has carefully prepared her audience by allowing them to see more of the truth of the situation than any one character can perceive. But a first encounter with this passage does not exhaust its ironic implications, and only in retrospect—or upon second reading—do we understand its relation to the total pattern of dramatic action. The point about such complicated irony is that it depends on a full *external* revelation of the characters' inner natures; we rely more upon what they say and do than upon the author's comments. In this passage, as in so many others, we are reminded of the novel's affinities with the best in eighteenth-century drama. The tripartite structure of *Pride and Prejudice,* dictated by the conventional three-decker form of publication, is similar to the structure of a three-act play, and we know from a remark in one of her letters to Cassandra that Jane Austen considered the volumes as separate units:

> The second volume is shorter than I could wish, but the difference is not so much in reality as in look, there being a larger proportion of narrative in that part.[17]

This remark reveals the dramatist's eye for symmetry, but the reference to "a larger proportion of narrative" is scarcely apologetic, and we must realize that Jane Austen's method in *Pride and Prejudice* depends heavily on scenic effects but is not limited to them. The first half of the novel could easily be translated into a play; here Darcy and Elizabeth are "on stage," joining with the other characters to dramatize the novel's psychological and social conflicts. Howard S. Babb has shown how Jane Austen plays on the word "performance" in the early dialogues, bringing all the implications of the word together in the great scene at Rosings (174–6) [II, viii], where Elizabeth's actual performance at the piano becomes the center of a dramatic confrontation.[18] But after the scene at Rosings, when Darcy's letter begins Elizabeth's movement toward self-recognition, the term "performance" quietly disappears from the novel. The first half of *Pride and Prejudice* has indeed been a dramatic performance, but in the second half a

[17] *Letters,* 29 January 1813.
[18] Babb, op. cit. pp. 132–41.

mixture of narrative, summary, and scene carries the plot toward its conclusion.

Yet this movement from the predominantly "scenic" construction of the first half of *Pride and Prejudice* into the less dramatic narrative of the second half does not lead to a drop in our interest, nor do we feel that the consistency of the novel's form has been violated. This is because the novel is unified by the indirect presence of Jane Austen's sensibility, and by the direct presence of Elizabeth Bennet as a commanding center of our interest. The shift from the scene at Rosings to Elizabeth's reception of Darcy's letter merely internalizes the drama; and the account of Elizabeth's changing reactions to Darcy's letter reminds us that Jane Austen has not renounced her right to record the inner life of a character with absolute authority. This is not to say that Elizabeth is a Jamesian "center of consciousness"; Jane Austen was too sure of her created world (and of its relation to the actual world) to efface her own personality from the novel, and from first sentence to last we are aware of the artist's command over her fictions. But her early experiments had shown the need for some technique that would counteract the novel's general tendency toward looseness of form by "focusing" action and psychological exposition, and in *The Watsons* she had explored the method of telling a story from the point-of-view of one character while reserving the right to qualify and expand that viewpoint through dramatic irony and direct comment. Such a method is really a compromise: it combines in a limited form the omniscience of traditional third-person narration with the immediacy of first-person narrative, giving the reader a sense of involvement and identification while simultaneously providing the perspective necessary for moral judgment. Of course, this method makes the exacting demand that the novel's central figure be perpetually intelligent and interesting, a demand which Jane Austen could only partially satisfy in *The Watsons*. But in revising *Pride and Prejudice* she created a heroine who could justify the form, and the result was a highly unified work in which the center of our interest is always at the center of the artistic composition.

PART TWO

View Points

Mary Lascelles: Narrative Art in Pride and Prejudice

"I cannot . . . conceive," Henry James says, "in any novel worth discussing at all, of a passage of description that is not in its intention narrative, a passage of dialogue that is not in its intention descriptive, a touch of truth of any sort that does not partake of the nature of incident, or an incident that derives its interest from any other source than the general and only source of the success of a work of art—that of being illustrative." [1] And, having dealt severely with the critics who like compartments and labels, he asseverates: "I cannot see what is meant by talking as if there were a part of a novel which is the story and part of it which for mystical reasons is not." [2]

This conviction of the integrity of a good novel—this impression that it must be unprofitable to study "plot" and "characters" separately—is strongly borne out by a study of Jane Austen's narrative art. . . . Whether we approach it in the first place by way of her presentation of character, or of her construction of plot, we shall discover the need . . . of reaching some central vantage-point, from which the "old-fashioned distinction between the novel of character and the novel of incident" (as Henry James calls it) is seen to be insignificant. For, "What" (he demands) "is character but the determination of incident? What is incident but the illustration of character?" [3]

It is not often that this can be said of those fictitious characters whose internal mechanism is of the simplest kind—characters to which comedy has always been hospitable. They are often curiously intractable—likely, when they are compelled to serve the main interests of the story, to do or suffer injury. If they have been introduced for the sake of suggesting some contrast, they will either give it an unintended turn—throw queer lights on the figure to which they are to act as foil, as Scott's gallant ruffians do on his heroes—or else lose all characteristics but those that serve for this contrast. . . .

"Narrative Art [in Pride and Prejudice]." From Jane Austen and Her Art by Mary Lascelles (Oxford: Clarendon Press, 1939), pp. 146–63. Copyright © 1939 by the Clarendon Press. Reprinted by permission of the publisher.

[1] Partial Portraits: "The Art of Fiction," 1888, pp. 391, 392.
[2] Ibid., p. 399.
[3] Ibid., p. 392.

Now one would hardly expect usefulness of Mr. Collins, a creature born of his author's youthful fancy in its most hilarious mood. "Can he be a sensible man, sir?" Elizabeth asks her father, after hearing him read the letter in which their cousin introduces himself; and Mr. Bennet answers: "No, my dear: I think not. I have great hopes of finding him quite the reverse." [4] Indeed, he is a being of some exquisitely non-sensible world, of another element than ours, one to which he is "native and endued." Whether he bestows his favour upon Elizabeth, pleased to contemplate the notion of her wit "tempered with silence," or whether he withdraws it—yet gravely explains that she is not excepted from his good wishes for the health of her family—he does not strain probability, as Sir William Lucas strains it by the simplicity of *his* machinery; he transcends it. And so it is not enough to exclaim, "No one would speak so"; and one is still too moderate if one protests, "No one would even think so"; for Mr. Collins is the *quintessence* of a character, in Lamb's sense of the word when he defined quintessence as an apple-pie made all of quinces. He does and says not those things which such a man would say and do, nor even those which he would wish to say and do, but those towards which the whole bias of his nature bends him, and from which no thought of consequences, no faintest sense of their possible impact upon other people, deters him. And is such a creature as this to be put into the shafts and draw a plot? Mr. Elton [in *Emma*], his nearest relation, might, and does, perform such a service, for he, with all his comic exuberance, is a being of our familiar element; but can it be exacted of Mr. Collins? It is, and with capital effect. As well as making his own contribution to the story, by the comedy he plays out with Elizabeth and her family and neighbours, he has to draw and hold together Longbourn and Hunsford; to bring Hunsford within range of our imagination awhile before we can be taken there (and incidentally to confirm Elizabeth's ill opinion of every one connected with Darcy), to draw Elizabeth to Hunsford when the time is ripe, and eventually to send Lady Catherine post-haste to Longbourn on her catastrophic visit. It is worth stopping to notice how unobtrusively this last incident is suggested: Lady Catherine, questioned by Mrs. Bennet, mentions that she saw Mr. and Mrs. Collins "the night before last." To Elizabeth, she opens her attack by saying: "A report of a most alarming nature, reached me two days ago"—the report of her engagement to Darcy.[5] We are left to infer a connexion between these two references; and then, after a sufficient interval for the carriage of a letter, comes Mr. Collins's warning to Elizabeth against "a precipitate

---

[4] *Pride and Prejudice*, p. 64 [I, xiii].
[5] *Ibid.*, pp. 352, 353 [III, xiv].

closure with the gentleman's proposals": "We have reason to imagine
that his aunt, lady Catherine de Bourgh, does not look on the match
with a friendly eye. . . . After mentioning the likelihood of this marriage to her ladyship last night," he has felt it his duty to offer this
warning.[6] Such are the care and ingenuity that Jane Austen expends
even on the broadly comic characters of her early invention. . . .

The problem which Mrs. Bennet presents is a little different; she
is not the sort of character that is likely to embarrass its creator by
uncontrollable vitality . . . ; Mrs. Bennet was "a woman of mean
understanding, little information, and uncertain temper. When she
was discontented she fancied herself nervous. The business of her life
was to get her daughters married; its solace was visiting and news." [7]
That, summing up for us the impressions of her that we have gained
from her first appearance, seems to dispose of Mrs. Bennet, to set her
where she must remain throughout the story. But we are to have a
good deal of her company, for her post is at the centre of the action;
and she must not become a dead weight. Mr. E. M. Forster, when he
divides the characters of fiction into "round" and "flat," brings his
argument to a head in this sentence: "The test of a round character
is whether it is capable of surprising in a convincing way. If it never
surprises, it is flat. It it does not convince, it is a flat pretending to be
round." [8] But it seems to me that this analysis does not allow for such
a character as Mrs. Bennet, of whose comic essence it is that she should
be incapable of any but her habitual, and therefore inapposite, reaction to life in all its variety. She must indeed surprise us—in order
to keep our response to her alive—but may surprise us only by the inexhaustible variety of expression devised for her unvarying reaction
to circumstance. And it is in devising this variety of form for what is
substantially invariable—for a Mrs. Bennet who is to be left as she was
found "occasionally nervous and invariably silly" [9]—that Jane Austen
displays her virtuosity, giving her creature the entail of Longbourn,
a theme of specious importance, to play her variations upon. We hear
of it first when Mr. Collins offers himself as a visitor, and Mr. Bennet
reminds his wife that this cousin "when I am dead, may turn you all
out of this house as soon as he pleases." " 'Oh my dear,' cried his
wife, 'I cannot bear to hear that mentioned. Pray do not talk of that

[6] *Ibid.*, p. 363 [III, xv].

[7] *Ibid.*, p. 5 [i].

[8] *Aspects of the Novel*, p. 106. He admits, however, some flat characters into
comedy, provided they give an illusion of intense vitality. Mr. Muir replies to this
passage (*The Structure of the Novel*, 1928, ch. vi) with a plea for the flat character
as the "incarnation of habit"—one aspect, that is, of the truth about people; but
this does not wholly account for Mrs. Bennet.

[9] *Pride and Prejudice*, p. 385 [III, xix].

odious man. I do think it is the hardest thing in the world, that your estate should be entailed away from your own children; and I am sure if I had been you, I should have tried long ago to do something or other about it.'

"Jane and Elizabeth attempted to explain to her the nature of an entail. They had often attempted it before, but it was a subject on which Mrs. Bennet was beyond the reach of reason. . . ." There we are, in the thick of it, knowing what is to be Mrs. Bennet's inevitable response to this subject, ignorant how its mode will be varied—though the close of this very passage promises something:

". . . She continued to rail bitterly against the cruelty of settling an estate away from a family of five daughters, in favour of a man whom nobody cared anything about." [10]

Mr. Collins, on arrival, is offered a sufficiently surprising variation on this theme: ". . . Such things I know are all chance in this world. There is no knowing how estates will go when once they come to be entailed" [11]—and contributes something to it himself by his proposal of marrying one of his cousins in reparation. And when this falls through—and, worse still, he marries some one else—Mrs. Bennet returns to her favourite subject with fresh energy: "How any one could have the conscience to entail away an estate from one's own daughters I cannot understand; and all for the sake of Mr. Collins too!—Why should *he* have it more than anybody else?" [12]

And yet she still has something in reserve for us: when Elizabeth returns from visiting Mr. and Mrs. Collins her mother asks her whether they do not "often talk of having Longbourn when your father is dead. . . . Well, if they can be easy with an estate that is not lawfully their own, so much the better. *I* should be ashamed of having one that was only entailed on me." [13] And so she leaves us with the assurance that, as she had been talking of this subject before the story began, so she will continue after its close, with ever fresh turns of absurdity, happily corresponding with the busy futility of her actions. . . .

Lady Catherine's part in the story of *Pride and Prejudice* is no less precisely planned, but the fun of it is independent of burlesque; for the execution of this plan is so consistent with the comic essence of her character, that not only her appearances but the very anticipation of them (since she is portentously anticipated) compose themselves into a pattern of comedy. The story is shaped by the original misunder-

[10] *Ibid.*, pp. 61, 62 [I, xiii].
[11] *Ibid.*, p. 65 [I, xiii].
[12] *Ibid.*, p. 130 [I, xxiii].
[13] *Ibid.*, p. 228 [II, xvii].

standing and eventual good understanding between Darcy and Elizabeth; and it is Lady Catherine's office to assist at the first, unwittingly, and at the second against her will: her active interference in their affairs—itself finely in character—is the determining circumstance in their coming to understand one another's feelings and their own. Its effect upon Elizabeth is direct and obvious; but what a pleasantly ironic invention it is that Darcy, who has alienated Elizabeth by interfering with her sister's affairs, and is by no means ready to repent his interference, should be roused to indignation and action when Lady Catherine tries to interfere with *his*. Her "unjustifiable endeavours," as he calls them, to separate him from Elizabeth, send him straight to Longbourn; and so, as Elizabeth remarks: "Lady Catherine has been of infinite use, which ought to make her happy, for she loves to be of use." [14] And with that most appropriate valedictory the pattern of her part in the story is completed, as though with a flourish. . . .

Pride and Prejudice is no less deliberately shaped [than *Sense and Sensibility*]; its pattern shows an equal delight in the symmetry of correspondence and antithesis; but there is a notable difference in the contrivance. This pattern is formed by diverging and converging lines, by the movement of two people who are impelled apart until they reach a climax of mutual hostility, and thereafter bend their courses towards mutual understanding and amity. It is a pattern very common in fiction, but by no means easy to describe plausibly.

Of the two courses, Jane Austen traces but one by means of a continuous line; that line, however, is firm and fluent. Elizabeth's chief impetus is due to Wickham; but there is hardly a character in the story who contributes no momentum to it, nor any pressure from without to which she does not respond characteristically. Her misunderstanding of Darcy is thus much less simple, much less like the given condition of an invented problem, than Marianne's misunderstanding [in *Sense and Sensibility*] of Willoughby, or of Elinor. Her initial impulse towards this misunderstanding comes, of course, from Darcy himself, in that piece of flamboyant rudeness[15] which I suspect of being a little out of keeping; but from this point on all follows plausibly. Darcy's more characteristic reference to his own implacability[16] prepares her to believe just what she is going to hear of him so soon as Wickham addresses her. And how insinuating that address is! . . . Wickham owes no more to chance than that first silent encounter with Darcy that stirs Elizabeth's wakeful curiosity; it is his adroitness that transforms curiosity into sympathetic indignation.

[14] *Ibid.*, p. 381 [III, xviii].
[15] *Ibid.*, pp. 11, 12 [I, iii].
[16] *Ibid.*, p. 58 [I, xi].

What provincial young lady, brought up among the small mysteries and intrigues of Mrs. Bennet's world, would not be flattered into sympathy by his relation of his own story[17] (so nicely corresponding with that of many heroes in popular fiction), or would criticize him for telling or herself for listening to such a private history? Or what young lady of Elizabeth's self-assurance would suspect that she was not to remain its only hearer? Henceforward his adversaries—and even indifferent spectators—play into his hands: Miss Bingley's insolent interference rouses Elizabeth's pride and clouds her judgment; Charlotte Lucas causes her to mistake her own prejudice for generous sentiment;[18] Mr. Collins, by associating Darcy in her mind with the idol of his worship, strengthens every ill impression; Lady Catherine herself, by answering to Wickham's description, confirms part of his story, and by her proprietary praise of Darcy[19] fixes some of its implications; and Colonel Fitzwilliam, by his indiscreet half-confidence, ensures that Elizabeth shall see Darcy's action towards her sister in the harshest light.

Meanwhile, Darcy's ill opinion of the Bennets has been growing, under the influence of these very people and events, until the climax of the ungracious proposal and refusal is reached. And yet, in the centre of this disturbance, forces have begun to stir, and, almost imperceptibly, to allay it. And this entails a change of course which is very difficult to contrive. The initial impulse must not seem to have spent itself—that would leave a fatal impression of lassitude. There must be deflexion; and this, for Jane Austen, means cause and opportunity to reconsider character and action. (Not conduct alone; she has little use for those casual encounters in ambiguous circumstances which are the staple of Fanny Burney's misunderstandings between lovers.[20] Even while they are drawing yet farther apart, Elizabeth and Darcy have begun to feel unfamiliar doubts; sure as each still is of his and her own critical judgement, both have come to question the standards of their own social worlds. Her mother's behavior at Nether-

---

[17] He is ready with a creditable reason for making a confidence of it (p. 80 [I, xvi]).

[18] *Ibid.*, p. 90 [I, xviii].

[19] To Elizabeth she "talked of his coming with the greatest satisfaction, spoke of him in terms of the highest admiration, and seemed almost angry to find that he had already been frequently seen by Miss Lucas and herself" (p. 170 [II, vii]).

[20] "Where . . . ," she says, "though the conduct is mistaken, the feelings are not, it may not be very material" (*Emma*, p. 431 [III, xiii]). She mocks the conventional misunderstanding in *Northanger Abbey*, when Catherine sees Henry talking to a young woman "whom [she] immediately guessed to be his sister; thus unthinkingly throwing away a fair opportunity of considering him lost to her for ever, by being married already" (p. 53 [I, viii]).

field on two uncomfortable occasions disturbs Elizabeth in such a
way as to suggest that she had not been embarrassed by it before; and
Charlotte Lucas's conduct shocks her. Presently, Colonel Fitzwilliam's
manners give her a standard by which to judge Wickham's. In the
meantime Darcy has been unwillingly learning to criticize the manners
of his world as it is represented by Miss Bingley, and—touching him
more smartly—by Lady Catherine.

> "I have told Miss Bennet several times, that she will never play really
> well, unless she practices more; and though Mrs. Collins has no instru-
> ment, she is very welcome, as I have often told her, to come to Rosings
> every day, and play on the piano forte in Mrs. Jenkinson's room. She
> would be in nobody's way, you know, in that part of the house." Mr.
> Darcy looked a little ashamed of his aunt's ill breeding, and made no
> answer.[21]

And so, even when the climax of mutual exasperation is reached,
Elizabeth's criticism of Darcy meets some response in his consciousness, his statement of his objections to her family means something
to her; and the way is open for each to consider anew the actions and
character of the other. What Darcy has done is now shown afresh in
his letter; this I do not find quite plausible. The manner is right, but
not the matter: so much, and such, information would hardly be
volunteered by a proud and reserved man—unless under pressure
from his author, anxious to get on with the story. And perhaps it may
be the same pressure that hastens Elizabeth's complete acceptance of
its witness; for there is no time to lose; she must have revised her
whole impression of him before her visit to Pemberley—revised it
confidently enough to be able to indicate as much clearly to Wickham,
for our benefit:[22] "I think," she says enigmatically in answer to his
searching questions, "Mr. Darcy improves on acquaintance." This disturbs and provokes him to further inquiry: " 'For I dare not hope,' he
continued in a lower and more serious tone, 'that he is improved in
essentials.' 'Oh, no!' said Elizabeth. 'In essentials, I believe, he is very
much what he ever was.' "—and she develops this proposition to Wickham's discomfort.[23]

The Pemberley visit is to supplement this revised impression of
Darcy with evidence as to character: Mrs. Reynolds is a useful piece
of machinery—but I do not think that the more exacting Jane Austen

---

[21] *Pride and Prejudice*, p. 173 [II, viii].
[22] But not, unfortunately, for Scott's. He may be suspected of skipping when he
says that Elizabeth "does not perceive that she has done a very foolish thing [in
refusing Darcy] until she accidentally visits a very handsome seat and grounds
belonging to her admirer" (review of *Emma*, pp. 194, 195).
[23] *Pride and Prejudice*, p. 234 [II, xviii].

of the later novels would have been content with her. It is more to the purpose that here Darcy and Elizabeth see one another for the first time in favourable—even flattering—circumstances: he at his best on his own estate (a piece of nice observation), and she among congenial companions. Lydia's disgrace has still to come—to give him opportunity for proving that he has taken her strictures to heart, to show her how much she values those hopes of a better understanding which it seems bound to frustrate. And Lady Catherine will involuntarily give the last turn to the plot by her interference. But these are needed to bring about rather the marriage than the better understanding. *That* had sprung from the very nature of the misunderstanding, from the interaction of character and circumstance. There had been, for example, something of wilfulness, even of playfulness, in Elizabeth's mood from the first, to promise eventual reaction: "I dare say you will find him very agreeable," Charlotte Lucas reassures her, when she is to dance with Darcy; and she replies: "Heaven forbid!—*That* would be the greatest misfortune of all!—To find a man agreeable whom one is determined to hate!—Do not wish me such an evil." [24]

Exactness of symmetry such as this carries with it one danger. The novelist's subtlety of apprehension may be numbed by this other faculty of his for imposing order on what he apprehends. His apprehension of human relationships, for example, may fail to develop, or, if it develops, fail to find due expression because he is impelled to simplify these relationships in his story in the interests of its pattern. To a contemporary it might perhaps seem, when *Pride and Prejudice* appeared, that such a misfortune was about to overtake Jane Austen.[25] *Mansfield Park* shows that it did not. . . .

E. M. Halliday: Narrative Perspective in *Pride and Prejudice*

Consider the famous opening sentence of *Pride and Prejudice:* "It is a truth universally acknowledged, that a single man in possession of a good fortune must be in want of a wife." The narrator seems to be standing outside the story, not yet observing the characters but gazing

---

"*Narrative Perspective in* Pride and Prejudice" *by E. M. Halliday. From* Nineteenth-Century Fiction, *XV (1960), 65–71. Copyright © 1960 by The Regents of the University of California. Reprinted by permission of The Regents and the author.*

[24] *Ibid.*, p. 90 [I, xviii].
[25] Not having seen a recent dramatization of it, he would not realize how much farther its human relationships could be simplified.

off into the middle distance for some reflections on life in general. But this impression does not last. As Mr. Bennet and "his lady" begin their dialogue, it rapidly becomes clear that the storyteller had them both in view when that opening generalization was made. It is an opinion, we find, that Mrs. Bennet would greet with a clapping of hands and little cries of joy—and one Mr. Bennet would send flying to the paradise of foolish ideas with a shaft of ridicule. The narrator ostensibly takes the responsibility for the opinion; but we see from the beginning that her observations are likely to bear an ironic relation to the views, and points of view, of her characters. This is our introduction to the quality of tough yet gentle irony that will control every page of the novel, making us feel a wonderful balance between sense and sensibility.

This artful control of over-all narrative perspective in the service of Jane Austen's irony is supported by a most subtle manipulation of point of view for the sake of the novel's unity. Even a sleepy reader of this book must be well aware, before he has read very far, that it is Elizabeth Bennet's story. But how does he know this? The title gives no clue, and Elizabeth is not the storyteller. The opening pages make it clear that the matrimonial prospects of the Bennet daughters will direct the action—but there are five daughters. True, three of them look far from promising: Mary is a pedantic bore; Lydia is an empty-headed flirt; Kitty is just empty-headed. But both Jane and Elizabeth are attractive and accomplished, and for several chapters it looks as if Jane's chances with Bingley will bring the central action into focus, with Elizabeth playing some subsidiary role. How is it, then, that by the time we are quarterway through the novel—say by the time Mr. Collins makes his celebrated proposal to Elizabeth—it has become perfectly clear that Elizabeth is the heroine of *Pride and Prejudice,* and that Jane is only a secondary character?

Partly, this is revealed by the sheer amount of attention the storyteller pays to Elizabeth, which increases rapidly as we move through the first eighteen chapters. This, of course, is itself a function of point of view. The storyteller chooses to gaze upon Elizabeth more and more often, and for longer and longer stretches of time. But the interesting fact is that this deliberate restriction of the narrator's privilege of gazing anywhere and everywhere is most stringently applied when the mechanics of the plot call, quite on the contrary, for attention to Jane. In chapter vii, Jane goes to visit Caroline Bingley at Netherfield. Mrs. Bennet's most sanguine hopes are fulfilled when Jane catches a bad cold on the way, and therefore has to spend several days with the Bingleys. But note that this is reported by letter; for when Jane leaves for Netherfield we do not go with her. The narrative perspective remains focused on the Bennet household, and particularly on Elizabeth; and it is not until Elizabeth decides to put sisterhood above gentility, and walks three miles across muddy fields, that we make our first entry into the Bingley household. Moreover, we see nothing of Jane until Elizabeth goes upstairs to nurse her; and even then we get a scanty glimpse, since Jane evidently is too sick to talk. By this time it begins to be obvious that the narrator is only slightly more interested in Jane than is the feline Miss Bingley, who tolerates her chiefly for the sake of Bingley's interest. Jane's relation to Bingley will be important in the plot, but much less for itself than as a necessary device to help build up Elizabeth's prejudice against Darcy.

Actually, the narrator's audacity in slighting Jane is almost rude. When poor Jane emerges from her sickroom after several days (chap. xi), she is nearly ignored. Everyone greets her politely, of course; but although Bingley "then sat down by her and talked scarcely to anyone else," none of this tête-à-tête between the two nascent lovers is reported. On the other hand, a word-for-word rendering of a most lively conversation including Elizabeth, Bingley, his sister, and Darcy takes up the rest of the chapter; but for all she contributes to the scene, Jane might as well be stretched out asleep on a sofa like the languid Mr. Hurst, who is also present but inaudible.

About this time we also begin to be aware that the narrator's increasing attention to Elizabeth and neglect of Jane is not simply a matter of direction of gaze. We are induced to see much of Elizabeth, and not much of her older sister; but we also begin to see more and more of the action, and of the other characters, from Elizabeth's point of view. In chapter x, for example, just before the one in which Jane becomes so remarkably inconspicuous, we are quite specifically encouraged to identify ourselves with Elizabeth at the beginning of the scene:

> Elizabeth took up some needlework and was sufficiently amused in attending to what passed between Darcy and his companion. The perpetual commendations of the lady either on his handwriting, or on the evenness of his lines, or on the length of his letter, with the perfect unconcern with which her praises were received, formed a curious dialogue, and was exactly in unison with her opinion of each.

We are not told that Elizabeth smiles, or makes any other outward sign of her amusement. The narrative perspective has penetrated to Elizabeth's consciousness; the point of view has become hers not only physically, but psychically.

By means of such skillful technical maneuvering, Jane Austen gradually forces the action of *Pride and Prejudice* to coalesce around Elizabeth, and we are prepared for an essential part of that action to take place in the intimate and subtle chambers of her mind. When we reach the crisis of the novel with Darcy's first proposal to Elizabeth (chap. xxxiv)—which, as a matter of structural nicety, comes exactly halfway through the book—we know that everything that follows must depend on her discovery of his true character. The groundwork is laid very shortly, in chapter xxxvi, which consists entirely of a searching analysis of Elizabeth's inward reactions to Darcy's letter of explanation. And the fact that her discovery is chiefly a psychological process, not an outward action, is stressed by her realization that it involves *self*-discovery. "Had I been in love," she cries (tantalizing the reader with the conditional), "I could not have been more wretchedly blind. . . . I have courted prepossession and ignorance and driven reason away where either were concerned. Till this moment I never knew myself."

Thus the management of narrative perspective plays an essential part in establishing the unity of the action: it is Elizabeth's story, and it is the story of her sense and sensibility rather than her outward behavior. But now an intriguing question occurs. If Elizabeth is to be the center of vision, why is she treated, in the opening chapters, merely on an equal plane with the other principal characters? Why the delay in establishing her predominance?

There appear to be some very good reasons for this, having to do with the use of point of view to help create suspense. The most violent outward action in *Pride and Prejudice,* perhaps, is Elizabeth's leap over a puddle on her way to Netherfield. Clearly, the suspense in this novel depends not on violent action, or even the threat thereof—despite Mrs. Bennet's nervous fears that Mr. Bennet will fight Wickham. It depends mostly on our waiting for Elizabeth to discover two things: that Darcy is in love with her; and that she is in love with Darcy. The reader must be led to suspect both of these things before Elizabeth does, or the suspense is lost. But if the point of view of the narration had been Elizabeth's from the start, the reader could hardly be aware that Darcy is falling in love; for Elizabeth, blinded by intense prejudice, never dreams of his affection. The storyteller therefore treats us to several direct insights into Darcy's mind in the early stages of the action: he begins by finding her eyes entrancing in chapter vi, and by chapter x is obliged to admit to himself that he "had never been so bewitched by any woman as he was by her." Once it is firmly established that Darcy is slipping, however reluctantly, the narrator can safely project the point of view to that of the prejudiced heroine; and from then on we rarely desert Elizabeth as the center of vision.

As for Elizabeth's falling in love with Darcy, it is something not accomplished until near the end of the book; but we must feel, surely, that it is something *begun* much earlier than Elizabeth herself realizes. To effect this, we must be able to see Darcy apart from Elizabeth's conscious bias: we must see him, almost from the start, as at least potentially worthy of her love. No doubt we begin to take this view of Darcy early, despite his snobbish behavior, partly because we know he is falling in love with Elizabeth. Since we have begun to like her very much ourselves, this stands to his credit in the face of her prejudice; it shows his discrimination. But, as we have seen, our knowledge that Darcy is falling in love would have been impossible if Elizabeth had become the center of vision too soon. Thus our respect for Darcy, which we must feel before believing that so estimable a heroine could fall in love with him, also depends on keeping the point of view away from Elizabeth for a certain length of time.

And what about Elizabeth's specific prejudices against Darcy? If there is to be an interesting degree of suspense, we must not share them wholeheartedly with her: we must believe, long before she does, that the foundations on which they rest are doubtful, so that we may anticipate her change of heart. There are three things Elizabeth seriously holds against Darcy: she thinks he has spoiled Jane's chances with Bingley; that he has done this because he despises the social position of her family; and that he has ruined Wickham's career without due cause. After she has accused Darcy of these faults and hurled his proposal back in his face, he writes her the long, painstaking letter in which he clears himself of the charges. And it deserves attention that most of the grounds upon which he clears himself have been objectively established, early in the story—established, that is, in a way that would have been difficult or impossible in a narration primarily from Elizabeth's point of view. We must be left free to observe these grounds independent of Elizabeth, so that the possibility of romance between her and Darcy can beguile us long before it consciously dawns on her.

Darcy says, first, that Jane never displayed any love for Bingley, so to whisk him away to London could not be thought of as injuring Jane's emotions—and if we look back, we find that the narrator has carefully established this in the early chapters. Jane is so excessively demure that even when her heart is fluttering with romantic passion her manner shows only genteel pleasure and politeness. Even Elizabeth admits this, to Charlotte Lucas, in chapter vi; but it does not occur to her (as it may to the reader) that Bingley won't see through Jane's decorous disguise.

Darcy's explanation of why he wants to prevent marriage between Bingley and Jane is that he could not bear to see his friend marry into a family including such uncommonly ill-bred persons as Mrs. Bennet, Lydia, Kitty, and Mary: and we, the readers, have enjoyed generous exhibitions of their behavior, objectively related, from the opening pages of the novel. Although Darcy's disapproval on this score is damaging to the idea of romance between him and Elizabeth, it is not nearly so much so as her false conviction that he considers her family social station hopelessly beneath him.

Finally, Darcy's explanation of his treatment of Wickham, while it relies mostly on family history, brings to Elizabeth's attention certain improprieties in Wickham's behavior toward her—improprieties that were wide open to the reader's view in chapter xvi, even though at that time they were lost on Elizabeth. This chapter, in fact, is a kind of tour de force of narrative perspective: the point of view seems to be that of Elizabeth; yet in spite of many insights into her mental reaction to Wickham, the reader can maintain a certain detachment of judgment because the bulk of the chapter is fully recorded conversation—and what Wickham says constitutes his impropriety.

Thus the eminent part played by narrative perspective in establishing the artistic unity of *Pride and Prejudice* is achieved only by dint of some very skillful modification for the sake of dramatic suspense. Through a delicate balance between objective and subjective, we are given good reason to anticipate, with delicious anxiety, that Darcy and Elizabeth will wind up in each other's arms; yet Elizabeth, from whose point of view the story as a whole is focused, does not begin to perceive this denouement until near the end.

Two other points about Jane Austen's management of narrative perspective repay study. One has to do with what could be called her "kinaesthetics"—the sense of movement imparted by the author to the story, and the way in which this sense is controlled; the other, closely related, is her selectivity.

Much of *Pride and Prejudice* moves at the pace of life itself: the action is rendered with a degree of detail and fullness of dialogue that gives a highly developed dramatic illusion. But note how fast the storyteller can shift to drastic synopsis when it seems desirable to step up the action and move on to a scene essential to the plot. When Elizabeth is waiting at Longbourn for the Gardiners to come and take her on a tour of the Lake district, she is disappointed by a letter saying that they cannot start until two weeks later than planned, and consequently cannot go so far on their trip. Our shrewd narrator, however, has no intention of making us impatient without a purpose, and disposes of a whole month in two swift sentences: "Four weeks were to pass away before her uncle and aunt's arrival. But they did pass away, and Mr. and Mrs. Gardiner with their four children did at length appear at Longbourn." Geographical setting is dealt with just as jauntily: "It is not the object of this work," we are told a few lines further, "to give a description of Derbyshire, nor of any of the remarkable places through which their route thither lay. Oxford, Blenheim, Warwick, Kenilworth, Birmingham, etc., are sufficiently known." And just two pages later we are treading the plush carpets at Pemberley, ready for the next encounter between Elizabeth and Darcy.

When it comes to selectivity, the filters through which the narrator of *Pride and Prejudice* habitually views the action are much more discriminating than those of any photographer, and they positively cut out much that is the stock in trade of the average novelist. What color is Elizabeth's hair? What did she wear at the Netherfield ball? What in the world do these people eat at all the dinners that are mentioned? What do Mr. and Mrs. Bennet look like? But the answers to these and a hundred similar questions it is the narrator's privilege to withhold: we must take what he (or she) chooses to give us. What Jane Austen chooses to give is pretty well summed up in her observation about Darcy and Elizabeth at the happy moment when Elizabeth finally accepts Darcy's hand: "They walked on, without knowing in what direction. There was too much to be thought and felt and said for attention to any other objects." Thought and feeling, and their verbal expression—this is the world of Jane Austen, so beautifully illuminated for us by her artistic control of narrative perspective.

Mordecai Marcus: A Major Thematic Pattern in *Pride and Prejudice*

Most critics of Jane Austen's *Pride and Prejudice* have justly praised the economy and control of its plotting, emphasizing the skill with which the relationships between Collins and Charlotte, Wickham and Lydia, and Bingley and Jane function, sometimes ironically, to bring together Darcy and Elizabeth. Many critics have also stressed revealing contrasts among these four relationships and among the individual characters, but no one has noted a particular and detailed thematic balance which emphasizes the value and significance of the adjustment between Darcy and Elizabeth.

Many definitions have been proposed of an essential conflict which

"A Major Thematic Pattern in Pride and Prejudice*" by Mordecai Marcus. From* Nineteenth-Century Fiction, *XVI (1961), 274–79. Copyright © 1961 by The Regents of the University of California. Reprinted by permission of The Regents and the author.*

is resolved by Darcy and Elizabeth. Mark Schorer calls it an adjustment of "the social scale . . . with the moral scale";[1] Dorothy van Ghent: "The difficult and delicate reconciliation of the sensitively developed individual with the terms of his social existence";[2] David Daiches: "Adjustment between the claims of personal and social life."[3] These definitions, which are virtually identical and most conveniently stated in Daiches's formula, provide a basis for contrasting the four relationships.

At the center stand Darcy and Elizabeth, whose struggles lead to a reconciliation of personal and social claims. Far to one side of them stand Collins and Charlotte, who demonstrate a complete yielding to social claims. At the opposite extreme stand Wickham and Lydia, who represent capitulation to personal claims. It is difficult to fit Bingley and Jane into this pattern because immobility, not capitulation or progressive adjustment, characterizes them until they are united by outside forces. They may, however, be connected to the pattern by noting that they possess traits necessary for adjustment but do not see this until it is pointed out to them. They are also related to the pattern by their inability to assert personal claims and to resist certain social claims, which inability results in passivity rather than in adjustment or capitulation. In the thematic structure they can be placed towards the center but below Darcy and Elizabeth, in a realm of impercipience, passivity, and chance. Thus Collins-Charlotte and Wickham-Lydia contrast to Darcy and Elizabeth through lack of integrity, whereas Bingley and Jane contrast to them through lack of percipience and strength. Some detailed analysis will show further significance in these contrasts.

The relationship between Collins and Charlotte presents a complete abandonment of personal claims in favor of social claims, but their individual adjustments are distinctly different. Collins seeks a wife so he may set a proper social example and obey Lady Catherine's wishes. Charlotte will accept such a contemptible man because he is the only alternative to penury and social isolation. All of this is readily apparent, but the situation is complicated by signs that Collins, unlike Charlotte, is incapable of normal personal feeling. His whole character has been absorbed by his social mask, and so he relates only his social self to other social surfaces. Thus Collins does not exactly capitulate to social claims, for he never recognizes personal claims, and he is blind to the fact that his own personal claims are distorted social claims.

[1] "Pride Unprejudiced," *Kenyon Review*, XX (1958), 88.
[2] *The English Novel* (New York, 1953), p. 100.
[3] Introduction, *Pride and Prejudice* and *Sense and Sensibility* (New York, Modern Library, 1950), p. xix.

A brief analysis of his combination of arrogance and servility will explain this distortion. Collins values only social power, and so he seeks security by cringing before his superiors. To his potential inferiors he is arrogant and rude, which behavior expresses anger at those who will not recognize his social power and vindictive compensation for his cringing. The portrayal of Collins's almost mechanical character in which social claims have become indistinguishable from character gives us little sense of the original process by which social claims can crush personality, but such a portrayal might introduce a more pathetic note than the novel could sustain.

Charlotte, unlike Collins, does show the process of capitulation to social claims; her relationship with Elizabeth establishes the fact that she has intelligence, sensibility, and integrity. Thus her loneliness with Collins is the central pathos of her marriage; for Collins has lost nothing by the marriage because he had nothing to lose.

At the opposite extreme to Collins and Charlotte stand Wickham and Lydia, who yield almost completely to personal claims. Their chief motivation appears to be sexual passion, but other motives are visible. Lydia seeks freedom and excitement. Wickham avails himself of a chance to flee his creditors, and he also seems to have some hopes for an agreeable marriage settlement. The marriage gives promise of a brutalization which Jane Austen cautiously suggests in her concluding pages, but again the pathetic note is restrained.

Possibly Jane Austen sees a greater failure of integrity in the Wickham-Lydia than in the Collins-Charlotte marriage. Collins's selfishness is so much a part of his almost mechanical social self that we see no possible alternative to it for him; and Charlotte's yielding to social claims and acceptance of loneliness with Collins may seem little worse than the alternate fate of social isolation. Wickham and Lydia, on the other hand, have personal attractiveness and energy, which makes it difficult to forgive them for recklessly discarding any balance between personal and social claims. It is interesting to note that Jane Austen implies that Wickham and Lydia, the violators of sacred convention, will be more unhappy than Collins and Charlotte, who have sacrificed all or part of their personalities to society. Collins and Charlotte seem assured of a more or less indispensable social equilibrium which Wickham and Lydia will lack. Jane Austen could not, of course, consider the probably greater sexual satisfaction in a marriage such as Wickham and Lydia's. But comparisons between the relative failure of these marriages must remain precarious, for Charlotte might have had the courage and integrity to reject Collins.

The relationship between Bingley and Jane provides the novel with less movement than do Collins-Charlotte and Wickham-Lydia, but it provides more subtle and perhaps more revealing contrasts to the Darcy-Elizabeth relationship. The contrast between Bingley-Jane and Darcy-Elizabeth enables us to feel poignant modulations each time we compare one couple with the other. Bingley and Jane possess personal attractiveness and dignity, social graces, and a measure of good sense, but they lack insight, strength, and self-confidence. Jane's diffidence towards Bingley and her quickness to believe that he has lost interest in her show inability to assert personal claims and to resist excessive social claims. Bingley similarly lacks self-confidence, and he yields easily to criticism of Jane's social position. If we cannot imagine Bingley and Jane acting much differently, we at least are strongly concerned and sympathetic with their weaknesses; we wish that they had the strength of Darcy and Elizabeth.

Unlike Bingley and Jane, Darcy and Elizabeth are deep and strong enough to hope for each other's continued affection even after circumstances have borne strong evidence against it. Also, they are able to stand up against excessive social claims. Darcy becomes willing to associate himself with the Bennet family (Lady Catherine's opposition is a much slighter obstacle). Although the excessive social claims which Elizabeth must resist may be slighter, they are not negligible. First, she must resist an overbearing verbal storm from Lady Catherine (which surely would have crushed a Jane Bennet), and then she must assert her claim to Darcy despite her realization of her family's true nature. Of lesser importance are her embarrassment in informing her family that she will marry Darcy and her pain in observing Darcy in association with her mother and younger sisters.

Contrast between these two couples also reveals dangers that hover near for Darcy and Elizabeth. Elizabeth could never act as do Charlotte and Lydia, but we can imagine her yielding to hopeless passivity. Darcy could not act as Collins or Wickham do, but we can imagine him permanently stiffening into the inflexible pride he displayed in condemning Elizabeth's family to her face. Such action would scarcely parallel Bingley's behavior, but the weakness it would display would have effects like those of Bingley's weaknesses. Most important of all, Darcy's and Elizabeth's differences from Bingley and Jane suggest to us the power of will which Darcy and Elizabeth develop, the ability to educate themselves which lies at the heart of the novel.

Several critics have suggested that Collins and Wickham represent real marriage prospects for Elizabeth, but this seems doubtful. Marriage to a man she could not respect would be impossible for Elizabeth, unless, indeed, she were taken in by a charming but dishonest man such as Wickham, but if she were long enough deceived by Wickham to marry him—unlikely and fruitless for him as this would seem

—her action would not represent capitulation to personal values but would be only a serious error of judgment. Although the Collins-Charlotte and Wickham-Lydia marriages help to dramatize the possible fate of a girl in Elizabeth's social position, their chief purpose is to show by contrast the desirability and integrity of the adjustment between Darcy and Elizabeth. Only Bingley and Jane help to dramatize alternatives which were significantly possible for Darcy and Elizabeth and thus to show the strength represented by their adjustment.

One might object that the Collins-Charlotte and Wickham-Lydia relationships provide excessively artificial contrasts to Darcy and Elizabeth. But had Jane Austen created two more relationships as naturally contrasting to Darcy and Elizabeth as that of Bingley and Jane, and had shown major defects in those relationships, she might have created large-scale tragic effects. One may lament that she did not do exactly this, but one may also doubt that her gifts would have preserved their present power and integrity had she abandoned her comic irony, or attempted to combine it with tragic irony.

In contrasting Bingley-Jane and Darcy-Elizabeth I have, of course, neglected most of the process whereby Darcy and Elizabeth come to understand one another, to modify pride and prejudice, and to effect a successful adjustment between personal and social claims. That aspect of the novel has been amply illuminated elsewhere, and my object has been to demonstrate the pattern and effects of the thematic contrasts among the four couples.

Charles J. McCann: Setting and Character in *Pride and Prejudice*

The country house is perhaps the most familiar landmark in Jane Austen's setting, and far from being merely decorative, it serves a vital purpose. Generally, it is an essential ingredient of her art; relatively simple in *Persuasion,* where Kellynch is an instrument of the plot, complex in *Emma,* where Donwell Abbey is the background of a central scene, and more complex in *Mansfield Park,* where the house serves in the fullest way as the background of the story. This is the inevitable consequence of the fact that Jane Austen carefully places her characters in just the proper symbol of their economic, social,

"Setting and Character in Pride and Prejudice*" by Charles J. McCann. From* Nineteenth-Century Fiction, *XIX (1964), 65–75. Copyright © 1964 by The Regents of the University of California. Reprinted by permission of The Regents and the author.*

or intellectual condition. In this respect the country houses in all
Austen novels, and especially those in *Pride and Prejudice,* are constant values—that is to say, each is a recognizable emblem for a complex of social, economic, and intellectual realities. Thus, the preten-
tiousness of Rosings reveals Lady Catherine, as the nondescriptness of
Netherfield does Bingley.[1] To the extent that she employs the country
house emblematically Jane Austen can characterize obliquely, and
in *Pride and Prejudice* as in no other work this method dramatically
informs the entire novel.

Taken together, however, Netherfield, Rosings, and Pemberley are
much more than three emblems of three separate families, that is,
three discrete images. And this because, while the emblematic correspondence is soon made clear in the case of Netherfield and Rosings,
the two lesser houses of *Pride and Prejudice,* the correspondence between Pemberley and Darcy remains unclear in the early stages of the
action. While the early scenes of the work are built around Netherfield
and Rosings, Pemberley remains in the distance; we hear much about
it, but are not permitted to see it. Two revelatory ratios are established early, but one quantity in the third ratio remains unknown.
Thus, while Netherfield is to Bingley as Rosings is to Lady Catherine,
the unknown quantity that is Pemberley creates a certain mystery
about Darcy. Existing as it does in this unspecified relation to the
action and scene, Pemberley serves as the basis of a suspense which
amplifies, parallels, and resolves with, the Elizabeth-Darcy story. In
addition to furthering action and characterization, the image of Pemberley, always with the support of the two other houses, provides tonal,
rhythmic, and rational unities, and serves as a symbol which makes
the story—as comedy—possible. For it becomes a symbol of a fixed
value, of a stable condition to which the heroine belongs, but from
which she is separated by immaturity, and to which she finally attains.

---

[1] Marvin Mudrick has the following to say about this relation of character to
setting in Jane Austen: "In Jane Austen's early novels . . . The problem of action
is personal; choice, or the illusion of choice, is personal. It is not Longbourne and
Rosings, but Elizabeth and Lady Catherine, who stand opposed: the individual
makes his own climate, and does not have to locate himself in any other.

"In *Mansfield Park,* Jane Austen abridges this freedom for the first time. The
individual can no longer act without locating himself. Place and group have, indeed, become central: the individual faces, not a choice of action, but a choice of
allegiance; and the action of the novel is a collision of worlds." (*Jane Austen:
Irony as Defense and Discovery* [Princeton, 1952], p. 155.) I agree with Professor
Mudrick that the *action* of *Mansfield Park* is a collision of worlds; I would suggest,
however, that in *Pride and Prejudice,* while there may be "illusion of choice," at
the same time worlds do stand opposed—but more on the level of symbol than on
the level of action. That is to say that one (*PP*) is more uncomplicatedly ironic than
the other, or at least that one (*PP*) is comedy while the other is not-comedy.

...tness has an analogy in Bingley's character, and a bland-
...y suggested in him as here intensified. In retrospect, then,
...ces to country houses in the beginning of the novel are
...d by ancient Pemberley, which gains as much ascendancy
...ader's consciousness over rented Netherfield as aristocratic
...s over nouveau riche Bingley.
...s, the second-ranking house of *Pride and Prejudice*, hereto-
...y casually mentioned, is appropriately introduced by Mr.
...effusions. The actual change of scene to Rosings, however,
...ly after modulation: description of Pemberley by Wickham,
...iniscences about Pemberley between Mrs. Gardiner and Wick-
...y interrupting the crescendo of praise of Rosings, Jane Austen
...interfering with the reader's anticipation of Pemberley; by
...ing that Mr. Collins wears rose-colored glasses, she prevents
...nfusing with Rosings what has been associated with Pemberley;
...ly after the standard by which to judge Rosings has been set
...in this oblique conversational manner do we get Catherine's
...e, one that we may to some extent trust. But even then, "It was
...Collins's picture . . . rationally softened . . ." (p. 147) [II, iii].
...Collins's view (the best in the Kingdom!) is of ". . . a hand-
...modern building, well situated on rising ground" (p. 156). His
...iring account of the glazing of the front windows, praise which
...es Elizabeth unresponsive, reminds us that Lady Catherine's hus-
...d was the original owner. The effect of this summary treatment of
...Rosings setting is to give the impression of a new, flashy estab-
...ment, a fit casing for snobbish Lady Catherine de Bourgh.
...Elizabeth is of course able to adjust unselfconsciously to the atmos-
...eres of Netherfield and Rosings because she is unimpressed and
...moved by either. This reflects Jane Austen's relative unconcern
...ith Elizabeth's reaction to these settings; her purpose is to create
...hrough dialogue a picture of a third setting, that of Pemberley, and
...y this means to point out the disparity between the reader's and
...Elizabeth's awareness of its importance. And this disparity, Jane
...Austen does not allow us to forget, is due to Elizabeth's present feel-
...ings about Darcy.

In the preceding discussion, I have suggested that if we follow th
logic of associating houses and inhabitants a dilemma becomes a
parent in the case of Darcy and Pemberley, a dilemma resulting fro
unknowns which call the reliability of the association into questio
If the process of association advanced in a straightforward mann
we ought to have a most cold, forbidding picture of Pemberley. A
this because insofar as we are close to Elizabeth we ought to think
owner cold and forbidding. (We are, however, somewhat prepar

Pemberley, then, stands for that "rigorous and positive belief" which, according to Professor Brower, balances the "sense of variability." [2]

In order to accomplish these various ends, it is necessary for Austen to mention Pemberley early in the novel. While it would not, however, be to her purpose to define the exact relationship between Pemberley and Darcy this early, she must imply a *close* relationship. This she does from the introduction of both, when the assembly at Netherfield discovers Darcy to be so proud that "not all his large estate in Derbyshire could then save him from having a most forbidding, disagreeable countenance" (p. 10) [I, iii].[3] Moreover, while the "neutral" company is aware of a relationship between man and house—an inexact one, to be sure—Elizabeth, at this time a little too self-centered, is unwilling to accept this fact with all that it necessarily implies. Thus, early in the novel Darcy's possessions help define Elizabeth's position in a subtle dramatic irony:

> "His pride," said Miss Lucas, "does not offend *me* so much as pride often does, because there is an excuse for it. One cannot wonder that so very fine a young man, with family, fortune, everything in his favour, should think highly of himself. If I may so express it, he has a *right* to be proud."
> "That is very true," replied Elizabeth, "and I could easily forgive *his* pride, if he had not mortified *mine*" (p. 20) [I, v].

Pride has reared its head for the first time, and in a context intricately associated with Pemberley. Without itself being the source of conflict, Pemberley serves as a focal point around which the lines of conflict are drawn. In the disguised maneuvering to win Darcy, Pemberley becomes the image to which characters respond with their own kinds of pride. Elizabeth's own self-defensive pride has already been clearly established. A little later, when Miss Bingley tries to denigrate her unwitting rival by suggesting the ludicrousness of Elizabeth's mother at Pemberley, she is attempting to arouse Darcy's pride by pointing out the essential incompatibility of the two families. At the same time that it does this, her attack also reveals her mean spirit and points out an implicit sense of pride at feeling free to associate herself with what Darcy represents.

At this point one is uncertain as to whether Pemberley is deservedly an object of pride; later we are to be convinced that Darcy's pride is justifiable, but even at this point there is a clear indication that Pemberley is already a norm: for if Miss Bingley's "queen of the hill"

[2] Reuben A. Brower, *The Fields of Light* (New York, 1951), p. 173.
[3] Page numbers refer to *Pride and Prejudice*, ed. R. W. Chapman, 3rd ed., in *The Novels of Jane Austen*, 5 vols. (London, 1952), Vol. II.

tactics are to mean anything, there must be a "hill," and that hill is Pemberley. Futile hope of opening a soft spot in Darcy's heart by flattery of Pemberley guides Miss Bingley's tactics, but her excess— and we are meant to be aware that it is excess—calls her brother's better social sense into play. "Upon my word, Caroline, I should think it more possible to get Pemberley by purchase than by imitation" (p. 38) [I, viii].

While this early conversation sets up Pemberley as a possible ideal, Jane Austen, by reference to Pemberley, cunningly uses this dialogue to delineate four characters. Miss Bingley's lack of honor and sensitivity—she is unknowingly but blatantly baring her meanness—and Bingley's bland and formless good humor are clearly revealed. It also captures Mrs. Bennet's vulgarity, and here is one of the pleasures of reading "Honest Jane": unsympathetic characters are allowed to speak the truth. It is Elizabeth, however, who always holds the center of the stage. We are never allowed to forget that she, in her innocence and pride, must progress to discover another kind of pride and perhaps even another more complex innocence—the one born of custom and of ceremony.[4]

Much of the suspense of the novel is dependent on whether Elizabeth will successfully make such progress. The brilliance of Austen's artistry lies in that we are able to follow so closely the landmarks in Elizabeth's development. The suspense involved, however, is not merely a matter of controlled point of view. For there is as much anticipation of discovering what Pemberley—and consequently Darcy —will be, as there is in following Elizabeth's progress. Let us, for the sake of argument, imagine a version of the story in which Elizabeth and the reader were permitted from the start to see Pemberley. Such a version could still present the sort of awakening we see in *Emma* and in *Persuasion* where the pleasures we are discussing depend almost entirely on control of point of view, but much of the effect peculiar to *Pride and Prejudice* would have been lost. To illustrate this quality of *Pride and Prejudice,* consider the following passage. Elizabeth is selecting a book from the collection in the drawing room at Netherfield:

[4] Howard S. Babb has noticed the irony of Elizabeth's position, and calls our attention to the fact that the dialogue reveals what deep motivation Jane Austen has implanted in both Darcy and Elizabeth. "Dialogue with Feeling: A Note on *Pride and Prejudice,*" *Kenyon Review,* XX (Spring, 1958), 203–216. Babb's argument makes an interesting conjunction with the premise of this paper, that the relation of setting (much of which is presented through dialogue) to action produces irony.

Charles J. McCann

He (Bingley) immediately offered
brary afforded.

"And I wish my collection were la
credit; but I am an idle fellow; and tho
than I ever look into."

Elizabeth assured him that she could
in the room.

"I am astonished," said Miss Bingley, "
so small a collection of books.—What a
Pemberley, Mr. Darcy!"

"It ought to be good," he replied, "it has
erations" (pp. 37–38) [I, viii].

It is not astonishing that Netherfield has so
that Mr. Bingley senior had spent so much
he had little opportunity to purchase an est
library shelves. Netherfield thus contrasts w
lowed home of generations, and thereby crea
some respects modifies the Elizabeth-Darcy on
to the minor one of Bingley-Miss Bingley, char
Bingley, and Darcy, and—since our informatio
hearsay—adds suspense. While it is surely imp
of view is Elizabeth's, the suspenseful quality
cannot be discussed solely in those terms.

The irony of Elizabeth's position, emphasized b
the setting, is already becoming clear. Although
be both subjectively and objectively "in," she is a
both respects. There is additional irony in the fact t
now subjectively "in" but objectively "out," furnish
of our advance information about Pemberley. Her
to the inside track, in remarks such as, "Do let the p
uncle and aunt Philips be placed in the gallery at P
52–53) [I, x], supply pieces for the montage of an im
that gradually assembles in the reader's mind.

All the foregoing allusions to Pemberley have been
the action at Netherfield. Although we know from the r
ion of its inhabitants that Netherfield is considered a
house in a neighborhood of Lucases and Philipses, it is sig
not one aspect of Netherfield is praised during these discuss
from Mrs. Bennet's suspect enthusiasms. The reader is not
about Netherfield except that Bingley would be willing to
five minutes notice. Indeed, the sharpest image we have of it
"charming prospect over that gravel walk" (p. 42) [I, ix]. This

92

nondescrip
ness alread
the refere
dominated
in the re
Darcy ha
Rosing
fore onl
Collins's
comes o
and rem
ham. B
avoids
suggest
our co
and o
forth
pictu
Mr.
M
some
adm
leav
ban
the
lis

pl
u
w
t
l

to believe otherwise by the ending of Darcy's letter.) But the house, as we have been led to imagine it, does not at all reflect what we know of its master, whose attributes, while they might include nobility and inimitability, certainly do not seem to number delightfulness among them. Further uncertainty arises from the fact that our chief informant about Pemberley has been Miss Bingley, who, as a very interested party, is probably not a reliable architectural correspondent. Our suspicions about the accuracy of her reports are naturally aroused, and, if our suspicions prove correct, Pemberley may very well match its so-far-disagreeable master. At this point, then, two of the anticipated satisfactions of the story are in doubt: finding Pemberley magnificent, and discovering its master to be compatible with his milieu. With more than the simple interest evoked by Pemberley in Volume I, the reader approaches the end of Volume II with real suspense due to the expected, but apparent lack of, correspondence between house and master. This careful heightening of suspense, added to Elizabeth's expressed anxiety, accounts for that high tension we feel when "To Pemberley, therefore, they were to go" (p. 241) [II, xix].

Volume III opens on the same note, *tremolo:* ". . . her spirits were in a high flutter." The tension only gradually diminishes in what is by far the longest and most elaborate piece of description in the novel. Darcy's home, whose beauty is confirmed by a specific comparison to Rosings, is found to be truly superb. Pemberley, in short, has met high expectations: if anything its glories have been understated.[5] And Darcy, if we are to believe his housekeeper, is quite different from what Elizabeth has been led to believe. Elizabeth's preconception, however, is understandable, for she has been influenced by Bingley's hints that Darcy is susceptible to influence of place and situation. Then comes the sudden meeting in the park, and after a period of continued suspense during the tour Darcy surprisingly and significantly shows himself gracious in the test of meeting the middle-class Gardiners. The housekeeper's view of him proves to be the true one.

It is obvious that love works upon Darcy to open and soften his heretofore inapproachably proud character. But he has been in love with Elizabeth for some time. Why could he not have softened before? Bingley, though typically indiscriminate, has hit upon a basic element of Darcy's character when he remarks: "I declare I do not

---

[5] The expansive style helps make this scene significant, "significance in this particular case being the *rational meaning*," according to Dorothy Van Ghent, *The English Novel: Form and Function* (New York, 1953), pp. 107–109. See, also, Elizabeth Jenkins, *Jane Austen* (New York, 1949), p. 233: ". . . from the point of view of his [Darcy's] position in the work of art that presents him to us, the background of Pemberley . . . is truly harmonious."

know a more aweful object than Darcy, on particular occasions, and
in particular places; at his own house especially . . ." (p. 50–51) [I, x].
His setting seems to be a condition of Darcy's being. This is borne
out by the fact that Elizabeth's impressions of him at Pemberley are
shaken when she next sees him at Longbourn, now at his most forbidding. This insight of Bingley's, apparently borne out by Elizabeth's later experience, seems to contradict what we saw happening
in the meeting at Pemberley. But there is no real contradiction—this
merely reveals how sensitive Darcy is to both setting and character,
and when either, as at Longbourn, is distasteful to him, he assumes
a forbidding manner. But at Pemberley, where setting *and* Elizabeth's
company are congenial to him, the forbidding manner falls away,
thereby revealing it to be a polite form of indignation. At Pemberley,
with those he cares for, he can be his true self. That Pemberley does
not signify Darcy's whole personality in a one-for-one relationship,
as setting does for the lesser characters where economy of characterization is necessary, reveals a degree of complexity in Darcy's character. Moreover, the fact that love does work upon Darcy further
keeps him from being pasteboard, and further helps keep him as
human enough for the nothing-if-not-human Elizabeth. Thus it is
not surprising to find Elizabeth at Pemberley responding to a Darcy
who has been softened by love but who is also (the context suggests)
susceptible to setting:

> Never, even in the company of his dear friends at Netherfield, or his
> dignified relations at Rosings, had she seen him so desirous to please,
> so free from self-consequence, or unbending reserve as now, when . . .
> even the acquaintance of those to whom his attentions were addressed,
> would draw down the ridicule and censure of the ladies both of Nether-
> field and Rosings (p. 263) [III, ii].

The significance of the subtle correspondence between characters
and setting is underlined by the fact that Jane Austen from beginning to end never fails to suggest it. After the marriage, Pemberley
is the home of felicity, usually open only to those who are compatible
with its true elegance and with the personalities of its master and
mistress. Wickham is excluded; Mrs. Bennet is merely an occasional
visitor; characteristically she is taken up with Darcy's town house, not
with his chief possession, Pemberley. Netherfield, a dwelling for
transients, is closed. Even the owner of Rosings must swallow her
prejudice for the privilege of visiting the home of justifiable pride.

This discussion can shed some light on problems that have inter-
mittently troubled readers of *Pride and Prejudice:* what is seen as
a sudden change in Darcy, and what seems like opportunism in Eliza-

beth. As for Darcy, his apparent change is neither implausible nor unexpected. This is not to say that there has not been an illusion of change—an illusion due to the reader's early, imperfect vision of Darcy. Structured as the novel is, the reader cannot have a true picture of Darcy until he sees him at Pemberley. For if we are to follow the logic of the novel we must see Darcy's setting before we truly see him. As for the characteristic forbidding manner, it is merely an indication of his sensitivity to company and environment. Once the environmental unpleasantness has been removed, Darcy reveals himself to be what he has always been.[6]

The possibility of opportunism in Elizabeth can never be dismissed. However, Austen makes it clear that the visit to Pemberley affects her deeply. And later when her sister Jane asks her at what period she was first aware of her love for Darcy, she replies, jokingly: " 'It has been coming on so gradually, that I hardly know when it began. But I believe I must date it from my first seeing his beautiful grounds at Pemberley' " (p. 373) [III, xvii]. Elizabeth's remark seems straightforward on the surface; she intends it to be a sarcastic but playful comment about her apparent materialism. Elizabeth, of course, feels self-conscious enough to be forced to indulge in such facetiousness, but she can only do so because she does not believe the remark to be a true one. In view of what Pemberley has come to represent, however, we feel uneasy and wonder whether our author here intends us to see beyond Elizabeth's view of the matter. Sir Walter Scott, in his well-known objection, misses both the playfulness and the irony and stresses the opportunism latent in Elizabeth's answer.[7] In doing so he seems to have intuitively grasped the intended implication without understanding the manner in which it is expressed. As a consequence, he makes Elizabeth decidedly too unsympathetic. Whatever truth her answer holds is due not to simple snobbism or cupidity in Elizabeth, although Honest Jane does not leave out the possibility of a hidden "normal" measure of either, and we would be wise not

---

[6] For arguments on various other grounds as to the consistency of Darcy's character, see Brower, above, Babb, above, and Philip Drew, "A Significant Incident in *Pride and Prejudice*," *NCF*, XIII (March, 1959), 356–358.

[7] "The lady, on the contrary, hurt at the contempt of her connections, which the lover does not even attempt to suppress, and prejudiced against him on other accounts, refuses the hand which he ungraciously offers, and does not perceive that she has done a foolish thing until she accidentally visits a very handsome seat and grounds belonging to her admirer. They chance to meet exactly as her prudence had begun to subdue her prejudice. But the youth of this realm need not at present be taught the doctrine of selfishness." ("Emma: a Novel. By the Author of 'Sense and Sensibility,' 'Pride and Prejudice,' etc.," *Quarterly Review*, XIV [October, 1815], 188–201.)

to despite the fact that R. W. Chapman labels this position "grotesque." Impure motivation seems inevitable in view of Mark Schorer's finding that in Jane Austen's world "marriage [is] a brutal economic fact in an essentially materialistic society." [8]

All this should indicate that Jane Austen's view of Elizabeth's motivation is extremely complex: more sympathetic than Scott's, more realistic than Chapman's. What seems to make this reading of Elizabeth's motivation so convincing is the fact that Elizabeth has been presented as the sort of girl who would not return love unless her suitor possessed those traits which Pemberley happens to reflect and foster, and then she only becomes conscious of being *able* to love Darcy since their meeting at Pemberley. Thus the prevalent motif of the novel is here once again emphasized. When Elizabeth connects the notions of her love and Pemberley she reminds us of the relation of character to setting, the structural system of *Pride and Prejudice* which allows Jane Austen to accomplish her end—to present ironically the maturing of a well-disposed girl [9] without, as in *Emma,* adopting an extremely related point of view. And here, precisely for this reason, she is able to accomplish her end with not necessarily more beautiful but with more mild irony than in *Emma.* Another solution would have been to follow the pattern of Fielding, and that of all down to George Eliot, that is, to use the narrative voice as the major control by which the reader could position the character. Instead, Jane Austen complemented point of view by using the imagery of her setting; and by submerging imagery even more into her dramatic texture by conveying it through dialogue, she produced, long before such a technique became common, one of the most artfully subtle uses of setting.

[8] R. W. Chapman, *Jane Austen: Facts and Problems* (Oxford, 1948), p. 192. Mark Schorer, "Fiction and the 'Matrix of Analogy,'" *Kenyon Review,* XI (Autumn, 1949), 539–560; "Pride Unprejudiced," *Kenyon Review,* XVIII (Winter, 1956), 72–91.

[9] The reader will recognize this skeletal statement of theme for what is intended: argumentation, without attempt to embrace all the richness of theme as it has been vigorously exposed by Brower, Mudrick, Schorer, and Kliger. The latter's essay, a profound relation of the art-work to its intellectual milieu, has, moreover, been suggestive for my purposes. "The governing idea of *Pride and Prejudice,*" writes Samuel Kliger, "is the art-nature antithesis. . . ." ". . . the art-nature antithesis is abstracted into a symbolism adequate to cover the adventures and misadventures which keep Elizabeth and Darcy apart in mutual repulsion at the beginning of the tale and bring them together at the end." "Jane Austen's *Pride and Prejudice* in the Eighteenth-Century Mode." *University of Toronto Quarterly.* XVI (July, 1947), 357–370.

Andrew H. Wright: Heroines, Heroes, and Villains in *Pride and Prejudice*

I. Elizabeth Bennet

At first glance, perhaps, the two elder Bennet sisters may seem to vie with each other for primacy in *Pride and Prejudice*; but Elizabeth is definitely the heroine: not only does she explicitly represent one of the words of the title of the story; she also quite thoroughly dominates the action—and, by comparison, Jane is a shadowy accessory. The relationship of Miss Bennet to Bingley, which parallels that of Elizabeth and Darcy, is treated much less fully, partly because it is much simpler, but partly because it is intended to be a comment on that of her younger sister and the proud man from Derbyshire. Yet Jane throughout the book has the unqualified approbation of Elizabeth, author, and reader—though we may, with Elizabeth, wish to speak to her with the following affectionate mock-exasperation:

> "My dear Jane! . . . you are too good. Your sweetness and disinterestedness are really angelic; I do not know what to say to you. I feel as if I had never done you justice, or loved you as you deserve." [1]

Indeed it is because of—not despite—her perfection that we must reject Jane as the heroine: the author's concern is with the complexity, the interrelationship, of good and bad—the mixture which cannot be unmixed. Jane is a simple character, but " 'intricate characters are the *most* amusing,' " [2] and Jane, like Bingley, is not intricate: she is heroic but minor—she is not a heroine. "I must confess," writes Jane Austen of Elizabeth Bennet, "that I think her as delightful a creature as ever appeared in print, and how I shall be able to tolerate those who do not like *her* at least I do not know." [3]

To say that Darcy is proud and Elizabeth prejudiced is to tell but half the story. Pride and prejudice are faults; but they are also the necessary defects of desirable merits: self-respect and intelligence. Moreover, the novel makes clear the fact that Darcy's pride leads to prejudice and Elizabeth's prejudice stems from a pride in her own

---

"Heroines, Heroes, and Villains in Pride and Predjudice." *From* Jane Austen's Novels, A Study in Structure, *2nd ed., by Andrew H. Wright (London: Chatto & Windus, 1961), pp. 105–23. Copyright 1961 by Chatto & Windus. Reprinted by permission of the publisher.*

[1] *Pride and Predjudice*, pp. 134–35 [II,ix].   [2] Ibid., p. 42 [I,ix].

[3] *Letters*, II, 297 (to Cassandra Austen, 29 January 1813).

perceptions. So the ironic theme of the book might be said to centre on the dangers of intellectual complexity. Jane Bennet and Bingley are never exposed to these dangers; they are not sufficiently profound. But the hero and the heroine, because of their deep percipience, are, ironically, subject to failures of perception. Elizabeth has good reason to credit herself with the ability to discern people and situations extraordinarily well: she understands her family perfectly, knows William Collins from the first letter he writes, comprehends the merits and deficiencies of the Bingleys almost at once, appreciates Lady Catherine de Bourgh at first meeting. Her failures are with "intricate" people who moreover stand in a relationship of great intimacy to her: Charlotte Lucas, George Wickham, Fitzwilliam Darcy. And the book is given an added dimension because it shows that intimacy blurs perceptions: intelligence fails if there is insufficient distance between mind and object.

Charlotte Lucas is "a sensible, intelligent young woman, about twenty-seven . . . Elizabeth's intimate friend." [4] But we very soon know that in an important respect she differs from Elizabeth—though Elizabeth herself does not know this fact. When, very early in the first volume, they discuss the possibility of an attachment between Jane and Bingley, Charlotte says Jane should make some efforts in this direction; but Elizabeth reminds her friend that Miss Bennet hardly knows him. This, however, does not deter Charlotte:

> "I wish Jane success with all my heart; and if she were married to him tomorrow, I should think she had as good a chance of happiness, as if she were to be studying his character for a twelvemonth. Happiness in marriage is entirely a matter of chance. If the dispositions of the parties are ever so well known to each other, or ever so similar before-hand, it does not advance their felicity in the least. They aways continue to grow sufficiently unlike afterwards to have their share of vexation; and it is better to know as little as possible of the defects of the person with whom you are to pass your life." [5]

But Elizabeth does not believe this statement:

> "You make me laugh, Charlotte; but it is not sound. You know it is not sound, and that you would never act in this way yourself." [6]

Why does she refuse to believe Charlotte (who will soon demonstrate quite shockingly that she means every word she says on the subject of marriage)? It is because a natural kindness and affection have blinded Elizabeth to the demerits of her friend; it is because, in the nature of

---

[4] *Pride and Prejudice*, p. 18 [I,v].   [5] Ibid., p. 23 [I,vi].
[6] Ibid., p. 23 [I,vi].

things, involvement (which is so necessary and desirable, in Austenian terms) carries with it the inevitable consequence of obscuring the marvellous clarity and depth of understanding so necessary to success in personal association.

There is no evidence that Charlotte misunderstands William Collins, but there is much to show that Elizabeth does comprehend him perfectly. " 'Can he be a sensible man, sir?' " [7] she asks her father rhetorically after hearing the orotund phrases of the clergyman's letter. Nor is she wrong. At the Netherfield Ball, after dancing with him twice, "the moment of her release from him was exstacy," [8] but she derives some consolation in discussing his demerits with Charlotte. The next morning he proposes marriage to Elizabeth (" 'And now nothing remains for me but to assure you in the most animated language of the violence of my affection' "),[9] and of course she refuses him summarily. Then she is flabbergasted to learn that Charlotte has accepted Mr. Collins's subsequent proposal of marriage to her.

> She had always felt that Charlotte's opinion of matrimony was not exactly like her own, but she could not have supposed it possible that when called into action, she would have sacrificed every better feeling to worldly advantage. Charlotte the wife of Mr. Collins, was a most humiliating picture! [10]

And now, for the first time, she begins to see Charlotte as she really is: and "felt persuaded that no real confidence could ever subsist between them again." [11] Elizabeth has learned something from this experience, as is demonstrated in her conversation with Jane not long afterwards:

> "Do not be afraid of my running into any excess, of my encroaching on your privilege of universal good will. You need not. There are few people whom I really love, and still fewer of whom I think well. The more I see of the world, the more am I dissatisfied with it; and every day confirms my belief of the inconsistency of all human characters, and of the little dependence that can be placed on the appearance of either merit or sense. I have met with two instances lately; one I will not mention [it is Bingley's "want of proper resolution"]; the other is Charlotte's marriage. It is unaccountable! In every view it is unaccountable!" [12]

Elizabeth does not give Darcy a chance—or rather she does not give herself a chance to know how she really feels about him. The famous first encounter is comically disastrous; it occurs at the assembly where Darcy says to Bingley of Elizabeth, who is sitting down: " 'She is tol-

---

[7] Ibid., p. 64 [I,xiii].   [8] Ibid., p. 90 [I,xviii].   [9] Ibid., p. 106 [I,xix].
[10] Ibid., p. 125 [I,xxii].   [11] Ibid., p. 128 [I,xxiii].   [12] Ibid., p. 135 [II,i].

erable; but not handsome enough to tempt *me;* and I am in no humour at present to give consequence to young ladies who are slighted
by other men.' " And as a natural result, "Elizabeth remained with
no very cordial feelings towards him." [13]

But at Netherfield, where she has gone to nurse the ailing Jane,
Elizabeth makes her extraordinary and attractive personality felt—
so strongly that Mrs. Hurst and Miss Bingley take an immediate dislike to her; so strongly that she finds Darcy staring at her.

> She hardly knew how to suppose that she could be an object of ad-
> miration to so great a man; and yet that he should look at her because
> he disliked her, was still more strange. She could only imagine however
> at last, that she drew his notice because there was a something about
> her more wrong and reprehensible, according to his ideas of right, than
> in any other person present. The supposition did not pain her. She
> liked him too little to care for his approbation.[14]

However, when she refuses to dance with him and says, " 'despise me
if you dare,' " he replies in unmistakable accents, " 'Indeed I do not
dare.' " [15]

With the insult of the Ball fresh in her mind, she does not like him;
she is even willing to overweigh the negative evidence, which now
presents itself first from Darcy himself, then from the plausible and
attractive Wickham. In the conversation at Netherfield, during which
Elizabeth makes her well-known remark, that " 'I hope I never ridicule
what is wise and good,' " she finds from Darcy that " 'My good opinion
once lost is lost for ever' " [16]—a chilling comment which she acknowledges to be a defect, but not a laughable one.

Then she meets Wickham, and finding him charming, very easily
believes his allegations that Darcy has behaved abominably, that the
latter has cast the young lieutenant from a promised living in the
church, that in fact both Darcy and his sister suffer from very excessive
pride. Elizabeth is vexed and even angry when Wickham fails to appear at the Netherfield Ball, again not trying to suppose that there
may be something to be said on Darcy's side. Even so, there are signs
that she willy-nilly succumbs to his charms—in the pertness of her
conversation while they are dancing:

> "It is *your* turn to say something now, Mr. Darcy.—*I* talked about
> the dance, and *you* ought to make some kind of remark on the size of
> the room, or the number of couples."
> He smiled, and assured her that whatever she wished him to say
> should be said.

[13] Ibid., p. 12 [I,iii].   [14] Ibid., p. 51 [I,x].   [15] Ibid., p. 52 [I,x].
[16] Ibid., pp. 57–58 [I,xi].

"Very well.—That reply will do for the present.—Perhaps by and bye
I may observe that private balls are much pleasanter than public ones.
—But *now* we may be silent."

"Do you talk by rule then, while you are dancing?"

"Sometimes. One must speak a little, you know. It would look odd
to be entirely silent for half an hour together, and yet for the advantage
of *some,* conversation ought to be so arranged as that they may have
the trouble of saying as little as possible."

"Are you consulting your own feelings in the present case, or do you
imagine that you are gratifying mine?"

"Both," replied Elizabeth archly; "for I have always seen a great similarity in the turn of our minds.—We are each of an unsocial, taciturn
disposition, unwilling to speak, unless we expect to say something that
will amaze the whole room, and be handed down to posterity with all the
éclat of a proverb." [17]

However, when she questions him about Wickham, he keeps silent—
nor can she understand him, as she readily admits before their dance
is finished. It is an artful irony of Jane Austen's that Miss Bingley
immediately thereafter tells her that Wickham is entirely in the wrong,
and Darcy in the right, in the breach between the two men. Elizabeth
disbelieves her for two reasons: first, because she has correctly sized
Miss Bingley up as an entirely unreliable source of information; and
second, perhaps, because she *wants* to dislike Darcy in order to avoid
any entanglement which will cost her her freedom. Nevertheless, she
feels mortified when she realizes that Darcy is overhearing Mrs. Bennet
boast that Jane and Bingley will soon be engaged.

In the second volume, the relationship of Darcy and Elizabeth is
resumed in Kent, at Rosings and at Hunsford, the parsonage to which
William Collins has taken his new wife. Everything is unpropitious,
so far as Elizabeth herself is concerned: she has agreed to visit Charlotte only because of the memory of their close friendship—"all the
comfort of intimacy was over." [18] Mr. Collins is just as senseless as ever;
Miss de Bourgh is " 'sickly and cross.—Yes, she will do for him [Darcy]
very well. She will make him a very proper wife' ";[19] and Lady
Catherine is quite as insufferable as Wickham has promised. Among
all these displeasing people comes Darcy, who adds to her annoyance
by looking confused when she asks whether he has seen Jane in London (for she suspects that he has warned Bingley off her); and, despite
his calls at the parsonage and their "chance" encounters in Rosings
Park, her prejudice against him increases, for she finds apparent cor-
roboration of her suspicions in the conversation with Colonel Fitzwilliam, during which he recounts the fact that Darcy has told him

[17] Ibid., p. 91 [I,xviii].   [18] Ibid., p. 146 [II,iii].   [19] Ibid., p. 158 [II,v].

of saving an intimate friend recently from a very imprudent marriage. And so she is bowled over when Darcy tells her he loves her:

> "In vain have I struggled. It will not do. My feelings will not be repressed. You must allow me to tell you how ardently I admire and love you." [20]

But she is more than astonished: she is gradually angered by the tone and implication of his remarks:

> His sense of her inferiority—of its being a degradation—of the family obstacles which judgment had always opposed to inclination, were dwelt on with a warmth which seemed due to the consequence he was wounding, but was very unlikely to recommend his suit.[21]

So—and not without recrimination for " 'ruining, perhaps for ever, the happiness of a most beloved sister' " and for his ill-treatment of Wickham—she refuses and dismisses the proud Mr. Fitzwilliam Darcy.

But this is not the end; indeed it is only the beginning of Elizabeth's very gradually successful efforts to know herself thoroughly. The next day she is handed Darcy's justly famous letter, written in proud tones and offering some new light not only on the Jane-Bingley business but upon the supposed unfairness to Wickham's claims. As to the first, Darcy says he thought Jane seemed not much attracted to Bingley, whereas Bingley was strongly attached to Jane; and furthermore, Darcy acknowledges an objection to Miss Bennet's family—two considerations which led him both to conceal from Bingley the fact of Jane's presence in London and to persuade his friend that she did not feel much affection for him. As for Wickham, the young Meryton militiaman resigned all claim to a living, in return for which Darcy gave him £3000 to study law. Three years later, the incumbent of the living, the claim to which Wickham had resigned, died; and Wickham, having lived a dissipated and extravagant life in London, sought it. Darcy refused, and Wickham abused him violently; but, more than that, sought Georgiana Darcy out, and persuaded her to elope with him— though the plot was prevented.

Elizabeth reads the letter with great astonishment and—at first— with little comprehension. She is, however, even more completely stunned by the account of Wickham, and her first impression is to disbelieve Darcy on that score too. But then, in reflecting on Wickham's behaviour at Meryton (especially with regard to his sudden betrothal to the rich Miss King), she is inclined to think it very probable that Darcy is telling the truth after all.

[20] Ibid., p. 189 [II,xi].   [21] Ibid., p. 189 [II,xi].

> She grew absolutely ashamed of herself.—Of neither Darcy nor Wick-
> ham could she think, without feeling that she had been blind, partial,
> prejudiced, absurd.
> "How despicably have I acted!" she cried.—"I, who have prided my-
> self on my discernment!—I, who have valued myself on my abilities!
> who have often disdained the generous candour of my sister, and grati-
> fied my vanity, in useless or blameable distrust.—How humiliating is
> this discovery!—Yet, how just a humiliation!—Had I been in love, I
> could not have been more wretchedly blind." [22]

In this dramatic moment of self-revelation she has the honesty to see
that there may be some justice in what Darcy has said about Jane,
for "she felt that Jane's feelings, though fervent, were little display,
and that there was a constant complacency in her air and manner,
not often united with great sensibility." [23] She has learned much from
the letter, very much indeed; but Jane Austen is too perceptive a
reader of character to suppose that all comes clear at once: it is by
a marvellous irony that Elizabeth is made to reflect, " 'Had I been
in love, I could not have been more wretchedly blind' "; nor, though
Elizabeth does know herself henceforth much better, does she yet
know herself completely.

It is even true that her attitude toward the letter is to undergo a
further change—when she has had a better chance to think of it with
some coolness. She almost completely reverses her first excited opinion:

> His attachment excited gratitude, his general character respect; but she
> could not approve him; nor could she for a moment repent her refusal,
> or feel the slightest inclination ever to see him again. In her own past
> behaviour, there was a constant source of vexation and regret; and in
> the unhappy defects of her family a subject of yet heavier chagrin.[24]

So, in a half-way stage in her thinking and feeling, she yet refuses
to look squarely at the consequences of a commitment to Darcy; she
still rebels against involvement. Nevertheless, her uncompromising
honesty causes her to realize that there is much justice in his views
about her family—all of them but Jane.

Elizabeth does not see Darcy again until the unexpected encounter
at Pemberley, to which she has gone with the Gardiners on vacation.
Presumably she has had an opportunity to absorb the lesson of the
letter; at least she is now more willing to believe good things about
him—from Mrs. Reynolds, for instance, who is the housekeeper of
Pemberley and has only warm praise for her master, whom she has
known since he was four years old—" 'and he was always the sweetest-
tempered, most generous-hearted, boy in the world.' " [25]

[22] Ibid., p. 208 [II,xiii].   [23] Ibid., p. 208 [II,xiii].   [24] Ibid., p. 212 [II,xiv].
[25] Ibid., p. 249 [III,i].

Already softened towards Darcy by such unstinted praise, she meets him by chance (he has returned home a day early) and finds him more civil to her than ever before, unfailingly kind to the Gardiners, and urgently desirous to " 'introduce my sister to your acquaintance.' " [26] She likes Georgiana, and after the meeting takes occasion to reflect on her own not very clear feelings:

> She certainly did not hate him. No; hatred had vanished long ago, and she had almost as long been ashamed of ever feeling a dislike against him, that could be so called. The respect created by the conviction of his valuable qualities, though at first unwillingly admitted, had for some time ceased to be repugnant to her feelings; and it was now heightened into somewhat of a friendlier nature, by the testimony so highly in his favour, and bringing forward his disposition in so amiable a light, which yesterday had produced. But above all, above respect and esteem, there was a motive within her of good will which could not be over-looked. It was gratitude.—Gratitude, not merely for having once loved her, but for loving her still well enough, to forgive all the petulance and acrimony of her manner in rejecting him, and all the unjust accusations accompanying her rejection. . . . She respected, she esteemed, she was grateful to him, she felt a real interest in his welfare; and she only wanted to know how far she wished that welfare to depend upon herself, and how far it would be for the happiness of both that she should employ the power, which her fancy told her she still possessed, of bringing on the renewal of his addresses.[27]

It is in the anti-climax of the first paragraph quoted (respect, esteem —gratitude) that Jane Austen is able to indicate something of the complexity of Elizabeth's mind, and the entire passage shows the continued resistance which she is still putting up against the release of her own strong feelings.

A crisis is called for, something which will break the placidity of her reflections; and this comes in the stunning news that Lydia Bennet and George Wickham have eloped; in her anguish Elizabeth blurts the story out to Darcy, who is most consolatory and kind. Nevertheless, when she leaves Derbyshire—as now she must, hurriedly—she is certain she will never see him again. She feels genuine regret on departure: and her feelings have ascended to another level.

Now the focus of attention shifts from Darcy and Elizabeth to Lydia and the conscienceless militia officer—the search for them in London, the self-recriminations of Mr. Bennet, the marriage agreed upon. Elizabeth has little leisure to reflect on her own feelings for several weeks. Then she begins to regret telling Darcy about the elopement, for now that Lydia and Wickham are to be married, she feels that the

[26] Ibid., p. 256 [III,i].   [27] Ibid., pp. 265–66 [III,ii].

first tawdry adventure might have been concealed from him, who would so strenuously disapprove—though no doubt he would not under any circumstances ally himself to a family connected in any way with the despicable Wickham.

> She began now to comprehend that he [Darcy] was exactly the man, who, in disposition and talents, would most suit her. His understanding and temper, though unlike her own, would have answered all her wishes. It was an union that must have been to the advantage of both; by her ease and liveliness, his mind might have been softened, his manners improved, and from his judgment, information, and knowledge of the world, she must have received benefit of greater importance.[28]

But now, she thinks, it is too late: such an alliance can never be— until she discovers that it has been Darcy who has been mainly instrumental in arranging the marriage between Lydia and Wickham, through motives which she must interpret in but one way: "Her heart did whisper, that he had done it for her." [29] But she still cannot quite believe that he would ever consent to be the brother-in-law of Wickham, even for her. Nevertheless, she refuses—with keen disdain—to promise Lady Catherine de Bourgh not to accept a proposal of marriage from Darcy: an interview which, as Darcy says, " 'taught me to hope . . . as I had scarcely ever allowed myself to hope before.' " [30] And so they are betrothed, at last.

But why has it been so much easier for her to like George Wickham? It is certainly true that, on their first meeting, he is much more polite than Darcy; his façade is much smoother, and his wit just as sharp. Elizabeth herself says, " 'I have courted prepossession and ignorance. . . .' " But there is a further reason, that she feels no danger of a permanent attachment to him; and for this second reason, she yields all too willingly to the belief that Darcy is what Wickham says he is.

She deceives herself: Mrs. Gardiner, who is much more perceptive in this matter than her niece, warns Elizabeth not to fall in love with the lieutenant. But Elizabeth promises only to go slowly. Nevertheless (and this, it seems to me, proves my second point) she feels not a single pang of regret when Wickham announces his engagement to Miss King, the girl with a dowry of £10,000. As she writes to her aunt,

> "I am now convinced . . . that I have never been much in love; for had I really experienced that pure and elevating passion, I should at present detest his very name, and wish him all manner of evil. But my feelings are not only cordial towards *him;* they are even impartial towards Miss King. . . . There can be no love in all this." [31]

[28] Ibid., p. 312 [III,viii].   [29] Ibid., p. 326 [III,x].   [30] Ibid., p. 367 [III,xvi].
[31] Ibid., p. 150 [II,iii].

And she is right: so she can afford herself the luxury of deciding, before leaving for Kent, that Wickham "must always be her model of the amiable and pleasing";[32] she can (or so she thinks) indulge herself in the imperception of denying to Mrs. Gardiner that Wickham's attachment discloses his mercenary motives.

The profundity of her mortification at knowing the truth about him comes, then, not merely from the knowledge that her perceptions, on which she has prided herself, have been beclouded by prejudice, but from the deeper reason that her relationship to him, because it has not engaged her much, has been able to afford the luxury of quasi-intimacy. Against clarity, in *Pride and Prejudice,* involvement is set: both are desirable, but each, ironically, works against the other—and the reader cannot believe that the marriage of Darcy and Elizabeth, however happy or beneficial, will ever quite close the breach between these two opposites.

II. *Fitzwilliam Darcy and George Wickham*

In *Pride and Prejudice,* hero and villain have prominent, interesting and convincing parts. Each is present throughout the novel, both attract the heroine, and both receive the marital fates which they deserve. Elizabeth Bennet is a complicated and penetrating heroine; the two men with whom she associates herself romantically must also be intricate and intelligent.

If (as we have shown) Elizabeth's prejudices are views in which she takes pride, so ought it be said that Darcy's pride leads to prejudice. But even this is an over-simplification: his austerity of manner, as we learn from his housekeeper at Pemberley, stems partly from an inordinate shyness. It is impossible, however, to explain away his famous remark about Elizabeth ("'. . . tolerable; but not handsome enough to tempt *me* . . .'"[33]) on the grounds of diffidence alone—nor, indeed, the statement that "'My good opinion once lost is lost for ever,'"[34] nor the first proposal to Elizabeth; nor his subsequent explanatory letter. He *is* a proud man.

One way in which Jane Austen delineates his character is through his relationship with Bingley. It is partly through this friendship that a certain completeness is given to Darcy's character. Although we are

[32] Ibid., p. 152 [II,iv].
[33] Ibid., p. 12 [I,iii]. This remark, however, does little more than show him to be out of humour. The reader should not make Elizabeth's mistake of judging him too hardly for it.
[34] Ibid., p. 58 [I,xi].

struck, at the very beginning of the book, with Darcy's rudeness and with his pride, we may overlook the solidity of temperament implied in his affection for Bingley.

Despite his early bad impression of Elizabeth, he is soon constrained to like her better: for, ironically, the heroine by behaving disdainfully to him, does just what is necessary to captivate him. Thus at Sir William Lucas's party, her refusal to dance with him only sets him to thinking of her attractiveness; her piquancy at Netherfield leads to the famous conversation in which Elizabeth, while acknowledging that " 'I dearly love a laugh,' " insists that " ' I hope I never ridicule what is wise or good.' " [35]—and from there to Darcy's increased awareness of "the danger of paying Elizabeth too much attention." [36]

The next appearance of Darcy comes when Elizabeth is visiting Hunsford, where she has gone to fulfil an unwilling promise of spending some time with Charlotte and William Collins. Besides the unfortunate first impression which the squire of Pemberley has made, there is now the insistent and plausible evidence against his character which Wickham has adduced. Elizabeth cannot understand the why of Darcy's repeated calls at the parsonage, nor can she comprehend the astonishing regularity of their "unexpected" encounters in the Park. And she is stunned by his declaration of love, and proposal of marriage (critics who censure Jane Austen for an alleged lack of emotion should re-read this chapter).

> Elizabeth's astonishment was beyond expression. She stared, coloured, doubted, and was silent. This he considered sufficient encouragement, and the avowal of all that he felt and had long felt for her, immediately followed. He spoke well, but there were feelings besides those of the heart to be detailed, and he was not more eloquent on the subject of tenderness than of pride. His sense of her inferiority—of its being a degradation—of the family obstacles which judgment had always opposed to inclination, were dwelt on with a warmth which seemed due to the consequence he was wounding, but was very unlikely to recommend his suit.
>
> In spite of her deeply-rooted dislike, she could not be insensible to the compliment of such a man's affection, and though her intentions did not vary for an instant, she was at first sorry for the pain he was to receive; till, roused to resentment by his subsequent language, she lost all compassion in anger. She tried, however, to compose herself to answer him with patience, when he should have done. He concluded with representing to her the strength of that attachment which, in spite of all his endeavours, he had found impossible to conquer; and with expressing his hope that it would now be rewarded by her acceptance of his hand. As he said this, she could easily see that he had no doubt of a favourable

[35] Ibid., p. 57 [I,xi].   [36] Ibid., p. 58 [I,xi].

answer. He *spoke* of apprehension and anxiety, but his countenance expressed real security. Such a circumstance could only exasperate farther. . . .[37]

Elizabeth's angry refusal marks the beginning of the great change in Darcy: he is humbled, though there is but one sentence in the letter which he writes to her, to indicate that he has been mollified: "I will only add, God bless you." [38]

Now he disappears from view, until Elizabeth, together with the Gardiners, visits Pemberley. Here Elizabeth's opinion of him softens slightly. And in fact there is a series of circumstances which disclose him to be a much more human person than she has previously thought him.

But this is not all: he behaves heroically, for he hastens to London, seeks out Lydia and Wickham, makes a provision for them, and all but drags them to the altar. These things he does not out of admiration for the eloped couple, but out of love for Elizabeth—which, however, he does not again bring himself to declare, until after Lady Catherine de Bourgh's interview with Elizabeth. This " 'taught me to hope,' " [39] and so he is able to propose again, this time with success.

George Wickham is at once the most plausible and the most villainous of Jane Austen's anti-heroes: he is handsome, persuasive, personable; disingenuous, calculating, and dishonourable. His appearance in the story comes just as Elizabeth, smarting from Darcy's disapprobation, willingly abrogates her critical faculties in favour of a pleasant countenance and manner. She all too readily believes the militia lieutenant's defamation of Darcy's character—though we, the readers, are expected to take note of the warning signals which Elizabeth ignores. In the first place, Jane Bennet declares:

"It is impossible. No man of common humanity, no man who had any value for his character, could be capable of it. Can his most intimate friends be so excessively deceived in him? Oh! no." [40]

In the second place, Miss Bingley plainly warns Elizabeth about Wickham, and indicates his relationship to Darcy:

"So, Miss Eliza, I hear you are quite delighted with George Wickham! —Your sister has been talking to me about him, and asking me a thousand questions; and I find that the young man forgot to tell you, among his other communications, that he was the son of old Wickham, the late Mr. Darcy's steward. Let me recommend you, however, as a friend, not to give implicit confidence to all his assertions; for as to Mr. Darcy's

[37] Ibid., p. 189 [II,xi].   [38] Ibid., p. 203 [II,xii].   [39] Ibid., p. 367 [III,xvi].
[40] Ibid., p. 85 [I,xvii].

using him ill, it is perfectly false; for, on the contrary, he has been always remarkably kind to him, though George Wickham has treated Mr. Darcy in a most infamous manner." [41]

Jane Austen does not stack the cards, but she is not averse to throwing sand in her readers' eyes: both Jane and Miss Bingley are, as it happens, perfectly correct here; but Elizabeth does not believe either of them, for Jane's unwillingness ever to be unkind does sometimes blind her to people's faults, and Caroline Bingley's careless, insensitive stupidity often leads to complete misapprehension.

So Elizabeth continues to think well of Wickham, and ill of Darcy —even when the former announces his engagement to Miss King, whose dowry is £10,000. This time the heroine ignores the testimony —or rather, the conjecture—of one whose judgment she has always trusted: her aunt, Mrs. Gardiner.

> "If [says Mrs. Gardiner] you will only tell me what sort of girl Miss King is, I shall know what to think."
> "She is a very good kind of girl, I believe. I know no harm of her."
> "But he paid her not the smallest attention, till her grandfather's death made her mistress of this fortune."
> "No—why should he? If it was not allowable for him to gain *my* affections, because I had no money, what occasion could there be for making love to a girl whom he did not care about, and who was equally poor?"
> "But there seems indelicacy in directing his attentions towards her, so soon after this event."
> "A man in distressed circumstances has not time for all those elegant decorums which other people may observe. If *she* does not object to it, why should *we?*"
> "*Her* not objecting, does not justify *him*. It only shews her being deficient in something herself—sense of feeling."
> "Well," cried Elizabeth, "have it as you choose. *He* shall be mercenary, and *she* shall be foolish." [42]

Although she is still unbelieving, however, Elizabeth will remember the doubts which she quashed in her early enthusiasm for Wickham— which, after all, arose partly out of her disdain for Darcy. Her big change dates from her second reading of Darcy's letter; then she excoriates herself for her blindness—though she cannot be expected to have guessed the full measure of Wickham's evil: his complete misrepresentation of Darcy, his planned elopement with Georgiana, his dissipated existence in London.

He gets the fate which he deserves: he marries Lydia, after causing

[41] Ibid., p. 94 [I,xviii].   [42] Ibid., p. 153 [II,iv].

great distress to everyone concerned, except the foolish young girl
herself. But, true to his character, he does not lose an ounce of aplomb.
On this visit to Longbourn:

> his manners were always so pleasing, that had his character and his
> marriage been exactly what they ought, his smiles and his easy address,
> while he claimed their relationship, would have delighted them all.
> Elizabeth had not before believed him quite equal to such assurance;
> but she sat down, resolving within herself, to draw no limits in future
> to the impudence of an impudent man.[43]

Darcy and Wickham are virtually perfect agents of illusionment,
and thus of the ironic theme, in *Pride and Prejudice*. Elizabeth is put
off by Darcy's rudeness; her vanity is piqued: but she allows herself
to over-emphasize his pride, because she comes so dangerously near
to involvement with him. She credits Wickham's testimony because it
is congenial to her—she missapprehends him because she wants to
avoid entanglement with Darcy, while in fact there is nothing to fear
from her relationship to Wickham: she is essentially indifferent to
him. Thus her clarity of perception, which she genuinely possesses,
contains the germs of its own myopia—ironically, when engagement of
her affections is threatened.

[43] Ibid., p. 316 [III,ix].

PART THREE

Special Pleading

Mrs. Bennet and the Dark Gods:
The Truth About Jane Austen

by Douglas Bush

Although our age has witnessed the superseding of tame traditional criticism by the anthropological-psychological method, the study of Jane Austen has not yet caught up with the new movement. Her critics still talk about "social comedy" and "eighteenth-century rationality" and the like. The revolutionary exponents of archetypal myth, who have revealed unsuspected depths in many familiar works of literature, have quite failed to see Jane Austen's essential affinity with Melville and Kafka.

That her mythic patterns should have gone so long unrecognized is startling evidence of the real subtlety of her mind and art, which have been so much praised for shallow reasons. Even a brief examination of the occult structuring of *Pride and Prejudice* will establish Jane Austen's claim to be the first great exemplar of the modern mythic consciousness. If conventional criticism should object that she was a notably rational person, and that she had read little outside eighteenth-century belles lettres, it may be said in reply that it is of the essence of the mythic technique that it should be at least half unconscious, that its operations should disclose themselves only to the anthropological critic. It may be granted that the various myths which underlie the smooth and simple surface of *Pride and Prejudice* are not fully and organically developed but—in keeping with the fragmentariness of the modern psyche and its world—are only mo-

"Mrs. Bennet and the Dark Gods: The Truth About Jane Austen" by Douglas Bush. From The Sewanee Review, LXIV *(1956), 591–96. Copyright © 1956 by The University of the South. This essay was reprinted under the title "Mrs. Bennet and the Dark Gods: The Key to Jane Austen" in* Engaged and Disengaged *by Douglas Bush (Cambridge, Mass.: Harvard University Press, 1966), pp. 20–26. Copyright © 1966 by the President and Fellows of Harvard College. Reprinted here by permission of* The Sewanee Review, Harvard University Press, *and the author.*

mentarily touched or blended in nebulous and shifting configurations; yet their presence in depth re-creates the values implicit in the outwardly commonplace situations of genteel village life. In mythic criticism the great thing is to find some semi-submerged rocks to stand on.

To the average casual reader, the first short chapter of *Pride and Prejudice* appears only to state the common theme of love and marriage, to set forth the character and situation of Mr. and Mrs. Bennet and their five marriageable daughters, and to report the arrival in the neighborhood of a highly eligible young bachelor, Mr. Bingley. Yet, from this brief and supposedly comic exposition, hints of the mythic and even mystic emerge. The famous first sentence, "It is a truth universally acknowledged, that a single man in possession of a good fortune must be in want of a wife," goes far beyond surface literalness. For on the next page we are told that Mrs. Bennet had been a beauty, and the single man in want of a wife reflects that desire for perpetuation of beauty expounded in Plato's *Symposium*. Ironically, although Mrs. Bennet has, in Platonic language, experienced "birth in beauty" five times, only one of her daughters is really beautiful; but it is this one that soon attracts Bingley.

Further, who and what is Bingley, the mysterious, ebullient stranger from the north who descends with his band of followers (his two sisters and Mr. Hurst and Mr. Darcy) upon a sleepy, conventional society and whom young people at once look to for providing dances? Clearly he is Dionysus, the disturbing visitor from northern Thrace. And who then is Pentheus, the king of Thebes who resisted the newcomer and was torn to pieces by the Maenads led by his own mother? Such violent data had to be somewhat adjusted by the author, yet it is hardly less clear that Pentheus is Mr. Bennet, the king of his small domain who is resentful of strangers and professedly unwilling to call on Bingley (his lack of tragic integrity is betrayed by his actually calling), and who undergoes a symbolic death in that he has no son and that his estate is entailed. Mrs. Bennet, to be sure, is not responsible for the entail, but she nags about it constantly, and she has urged her husband to cultivate Bingley, so that she must be a surrogate for Pentheus' Maenad mother. Bingley's fortune is a patent transliteration of the ivy and wine of Dionysus (the family money had been acquired in trade, undoubtedly distilling); and his sudden, unexplained comings and goings correspond to the epiphanies of the god. The mythic character of Darcy and of his relation to Bingley is less certain. However, his dominating personality and his initial blindness to the charms of Elizabeth Bennet suggest the blind seer Tiresias as the mentor of Dionysus-Bingley. (I pass by the obvious homosexuality;

on this level the two men are Hercules and Hylas.) Thus the simple persons and incidents of the novel take on from the start richly evocative and even sinister connotations.

As the story proceeds and tensions develop, the mythic pattern, and with it some individual roles, undergo subtle transformations; one myth shades into another. The once pretty Mrs. Bennet, whose sole concern is to get her daughters married, is an embodiment of the unthinking life-force that works through women, and she is Dionysiac in her devotion to Bingley. Her motherhood and her earthy mentality might at first suggest identification with the Earth Goddess, but one explicit clue indicates that she is the goddess of love, born of the sea —she is a native of Meryton, the town of *mare,* the sea. On this new level, Mr. Bennet is more complex and obscure, because in projecting him Miss Austen uses not so much the orthodox and familiar myth of Venus and Adonis but some Renaissance variations of it. On the one hand, in his cool indifference to his emotional wife and in his desire to be left alone in his library, Mr. Bennet is the cold Adonis, intent on his hunting, of Shakespeare's poem. On the other hand, Jane Austen fuses with this conception the Neoplatonic symbolism of Spenser's "Garden of Adonis": as an intellectual, and the parent of five daughters, Mr. Bennet is Spenser's Adonis, "the father of all Forms," and Mrs. Bennet is Spenser's Venus, simply unformed Matter. Whatever skepticism conventional scholarship may have concerning some of these interpretations, no one could dispute this last point.

But the security of Venus and Adonis is threatened (and will eventually be destroyed) by the Boar. In Jane Austen's multiple layers of meaning, the Boar is the entail, which comes into force with Mr. Bennet's death and which is personified in his heir, Rev. Mr. Collins. We have here what is perhaps the most striking mythic ambiguity in the book: Mr. Collins is both the Boar and the Bore (and his clerical status adds a further though unexploited element of traditional ritualism). Mr. Collins is in fact the axis of several polarities.

As if this interweaving of mythic patterns were not complex enough, the same pattern, with new features added, is worked out on another level and takes shape as the central figure in the carpet. The older Venus and Adonis are partly paralleled in a younger Venus and Adonis, Elizabeth and the initially proud and indifferent Darcy; but this second version operates in a vein of paradox. Mr. Bennet had in his youth been allured by a pretty face and had later discovered the stupidity behind it; Darcy, at first cold and then attracted by beauty, discovers the spirit and charm that go with it and falls deeply in love. Elizabeth, though misled for a time by the specious Wickham (a sort of Anteros), comes to love Darcy in her turn. But the security of the young pair's new relation is threatened by a variety of circumstances and most explicitly by a new Boar-Bore, not now Mr. Collins but his patroness, Lady Catherine (who has also some Gorgonish traits). Mr. Collins, like the mythical boar, while really killing had only sought to kiss (he proposed to Elizabeth); Lady Catherine, seeking to kill the relation between her nephew Darcy and Elizabeth, instead brings about his renewed proposal and acceptance. Some of these features of the design have, it is true, been noticed in conventional criticism, but only on the personal and social level; the deeper dimensions and reverberations have been completely missed.

There are many particulars one would like to go into, for instance, Elizabeth's uncle, Mr. Gardiner, whom Darcy so unexpectedly invites to fish on his estate: what is Mr. Gardiner's relation to the Fisher King, and what of the veiled phallicism in the allusion to fishing tackle? But only one other thread in the variegated web of complexity can be touched upon, the most central of all archetypal myths, the theme of death and rebirth. Jane Austen's heavy reliance upon this is all the more remarkable because she is commonly said to avoid the subject of death altogether; she never has a principal character die and only rarely reports such remote deaths as may contribute to the plot. But the real reason now becomes apparent: she did not deal with the subject in ordinary ways simply because her stories of young love are set against a dark mythic background of death. In *Pride and Prejudice* hints of mortality appear at the very beginning, in such place-names as Longbourn ("man goeth to his long home"; "The undiscover'd country from whose bourn No traveller returns") and Netherfield (the nether or lower world). There is a recurrent stress on physical frailty: Kitty Bennet has spells of coughing; Jane Bennet falls ill at Netherfield; Anne de Bourgh is sickly; and there is a whole crowd of adults whose parents are dead; etc. We have already observed the insistent significance of the entail and Mr. Collins, who will inherit the estate when Mr. Bennet dies. In proposing to Elizabeth, the magnanimous Mr. Collins says that he knows she will, after her mother's death, have no more than a thousand pounds in the four per cents. Such hieroglyphics of pain and death, both mythic and worldly, are reinforced by the process of the seasons. The book opens in early autumn, and in this season of harvest and death there is the ritual dance, which, ominously, takes place at Netherfield, Bingley's house. It is during the late autumn and winter that blows fall upon the Bennets—Mr. Collins' unhappy visit, Bingley's departure and abandoning of Jane Bennet and her heavy disappointment and Elizabeth's sympathy for her. The worst blow, Lydia's elopement with Wickham (note, by the way, the ancient view of the shallow, sensual quality of Lydian music), does occur in the summer, but it is this event that sets everything in motion toward rebirth, or what is crudely called a happy ending. Darcy—now a saving Hercules —rescues Lydia and wins Elizabeth; Dionysus-Bingley returns and is restored to Jane; and Mrs. Bennet, again a radiant Venus, rises from the depths in a foam of rejoicing.

Almost all the characters and incidents of the novel, under close scrutiny, will yield their mythic overtones, but perhaps enough has been said here to stimulate a critic who has the time and the insight for fuller investigation. The subject of archetypal myth in Jane Austen needs a book, and will doubtless get one.

Chronology of Important Dates

Jane Austen	The Age

1775 Jane Austen born.

        1776 U. S. declares independence.

        1789 French Revolution.

        1794 Executions of Danton and Robespierre; Paine's *Age of Reason*.

1797 *First Impressions* (original of *Pride and Prejudice*) completed; first version of *Sense and Sensibility* begun.

        1798 Wordsworth's and Coleridge's *Lyrical Ballads*.

1801 Jane Austen settles in Bath.

1803 First version of *Northanger Abbey* (called *Susan*) accepted for publication, but never appears.

        1804 Napoleon proclaimed Emperor.

1806 Jane Austen moves to Southampton.   **1806** Death of Pitt.

1809 Jane Austen settles at Chawton.

        1810 Scott's *Lady of the Lake*.

1811 *Sense and Sensibility* published.

1811 Prince of Wales (later George IV) made Regent.

1812 Napoleon in Russia; England at war with U. S.; Byron's *Childe Harold* (I and II).

1813 *Pride and Prejudice* published.

1813 Byron's *Bride of Abydos* and *Giaour,* Shelley's *Queen Mab.*

1814 *Mansfield Park* published.

1814 American war ends; Wordsworth's *Excursion,* Scott's *Waverley.*

1815 *Emma* published; MS of *Northanger Abbey* bought back from publisher.

1815 Battle of Waterloo.

1817 Jane Austen dies.

1817 Keats's *Poems.*

1818 *Persuasion* published in tandem with *Northanger Abbey.*

1818 Karl Marx born; Keats's *Endymion.*

Notes on the Editor and Contributors

E. RUBINSTEIN, the editor of this volume, is Assistant Professor in the Division of Humanities of Richmond College of the City University of New York. His *Jane Austen's Novels: The Metaphor of Rank* is being published by the University of Wisconsin Press in its *Literary Monographs* series, and he has published articles on Shakespeare, George Eliot, and Nabokov, in addition to those concerning Jane Austen.

REUBEN A. BROWER, Professor of English at Harvard University, is the author of books on Alexander Pope and Robert Frost.

DOUGLAS BUSH was for many years Professor of English at Harvard University. Among his numerous volumes is *English Literature in the Earlier Seventeenth Century* for the Oxford History of English Literature.

E. M. HALLIDAY, who has contributed critical articles on Ernest Hemingway to various journals, is an editor with the American Heritage Publishing Company.

SAMUEL KLIGER is Senior Editor in the Higher Education Department of Silver Burdett Company. His study of seventeenth- and eighteenth-century intellectual history, *The Goths in England,* appeared in 1952.

MARY LASCELLES has been Honorary Fellow of Somerville College, Oxford, since 1967. Her book on Shakespeare's *Measure for Measure* appeared in 1953.

A. WALTON LITZ is Professor of English at Princeton University. He has published a book on James Joyce in addition to his study of Jane Austen.

CHARLES J. MCCANN is presently Chairman of the English Department at Central Washington College.

MORDECAI MARCUS is Associate Professor of English at the University of Nebraska. He has published critical articles on several English and American writers.

The late DOROTHY VAN GHENT was one of America's most influential critics of the novel. She taught last at the State University of New York at Buffalo.

ANDREW H. WRIGHT, Professor of English at the University of California, San Diego, is the author of *Henry Fielding, Mask and Feast*.

Selected Bibliography

Babb, Howard S., *Jane Austen's Novels: the Fabric of Dialogue*. Columbus: Ohio University Press, 1962. Pages 113–44 examine the uses of conversation in *Pride and Prejudice*.

Cady, Joseph, and Ian Watt, "Jane Austen's Critics," *Critical Quarterly*, V (1963), 49–63. The best succinct study of Jane Austen's reputation from her time to ours.

Craik, W. A., *Jane Austen: The Six Novels*. London: Methuen & Co. Ltd., 1965. The discussion of *Pride and Prejudice* on pages 62 to 90 raises some basic compositional questions.

Garrod, H. W., "Jane Austen, a Depreciation," *Transactions of the Royal Society of Literature*, VIII (1928), 21–40. The classic statement of how not to like Jane Austen.

Harding, D. W., "Regulated Hatred: An Aspect of the Work of Jane Austen," *Scrutiny*, VIII (1940), 346–62. One of the first open attacks on the traditional view of Jane Austen; by its own admission "deliberately lop-sided," but still provocative.

Mudrick, Marvin, *Jane Austen: Irony as Defense and Discovery*. Princeton, N. J.: Princeton University Press, 1952. *Pride and Prejudice* is discussed on pages 94 to 126 of this major book. Mudrick is valuable not only for his own insights but for the arguments he provokes. One charge to be borne in mind when reading him is that his notion of "irony" in general and of Jane Austen's irony in particular is perhaps too limited and arbitrary.

Schorer, Mark. "Pride Unprejudiced," *The Kenyon Review* XVIII (1956), 72–91. Perhaps the best introduction to the world of the novel.

TWENTIETH CENTURY
INTERPRETATIONS

Maynard Mack, *Series Editor*
Yale University

NOW AVAILABLE
Collections of Critical Essays
ON

(continued on next page)

(continued from previous page)

KEATS'S ODES
LORD JIM
MUCH ADO ABOUT NOTHING
OEDIPUS REX
THE OLD MAN AND THE SEA
PAMELA
THE PLAYBOY OF THE WESTERN WORLD
THE PORTRAIT OF A LADY
A PORTRAIT OF THE ARTIST AS A YOUNG MAN
PRIDE AND PREJUDICE
THE RAPE OF THE LOCK
THE RIME OF THE ANCIENT MARINER
ROBINSON CRUSOE
SAMSON AGONISTES
THE SCARLET LETTER
SIR GAWAIN AND THE GREEN KNIGHT
THE SOUND AND THE FURY
THE TEMPEST
TOM JONES
TWELFTH NIGHT
UTOPIA
WALDEN
THE WASTE LAND
WUTHERING HEIGHTS